Unstuck

**10 Proven Strategies for Breaking Through the
Barriers to Small Business Growth**

Steve Woodruff

Terry Lancaster

Juliana Stachurski

Steve Byington

Terry Luker

Thom Coats

Kayla Barrett

Jim Bob Howard

Cindy Beresh-Bryant

Craig Paxson

CONTENTS

CONTENTS

Introduction

"Stuck" happens.

Every business gets stuck from time to time. We fantasize about running up the smooth, upward trajectory of growth—but there are hurdles, there are setbacks, and there are pits of quicksand along the way.

How we launch and build momentum may work for a season, but change and complexity materialize, throwing fistfuls of sand into the gearbox.

In short, growing pains are a normal part of running a business. Who knew there were so many ways to get bogged down by people, process, financial, and marketing issues?

If your growth trajectory is stalling out, welcome to the 99% club. Stuck happens. The key to success is to get *unstuck* as quickly as possible.

With over 235 years of combined business experience, the authors of this guidebook encountered many of the same hurdles you are facing right now. By pooling those decades of practical knowledge and addressing the common barriers facing business leaders, we hope to provide you with the keys to unlock your company's growth potential.

Industry Guides

Every company faces technology challenges in our software-driven world. Thom Coats demonstrates how technology can effectively liberate your time and effort instead of draining it away.

The online world is an ever-increasing engine of growth for most companies. While the digital landscape can be complex, there are tremendous opportunities for every small business. Terry Lancaster and Juliana Stachurski reveal how you can employ online strategies to generate leads and create an army of clients who trust your business before the first handshake.

Networking, of course, is the lifeblood for much of our business growth, yet many don't know how to strategically nurture beneficial connections. Jim Bob Howard helps you discover the hidden power of your network and find the array of people you need.

Every company grows best through referrals, but, in many cases, business professionals lose opportunities through a "failure to communicate." Steve Woodruff explains how to achieve message clarity and make your business referral-ready.

What growing company doesn't need to continually evaluate and improve its financial situation? Financial experts Steve Byington and Terry Luker illustrate how to make sure your cash flow matches the current (and future) needs of the business.

Growing a company means building an organization—what does success look like when facing the inevitable personnel issues? Cindy Beresh-Bryant discusses how to build a positive organizational culture (the OC Equation) that will attract and retain top talent. Kayla Barrett addresses the personnel/performance gridlock that inhibits organizational momentum.

Sometimes the key to fresh growth is generating new ideas. There is a process for that—Craig Paxson shares perspectives and tools to help your company bring productive ideas to the surface.

No volume like this one can address every single business challenge in a complex and evolving marketplace. However, there are a number of common ways for businesses to get stuck, and our hope is that you will find some gems in these pages that address your specific growing pains.

Stuck happens. Now let's get Unstuck!

> — Steve Woodruff, Clarity Consultant (aka The King of Clarity)

1

Overcome Your Biggest Competitor – With Clarity

Nobody's listening to your message.

I'm sorry to be the bearer of bad tidings, but you have a lot of competition out there for the attention of your customers.

You do good work. You have some happy customers. You should be killing it by now.

Customers should be flocking to you. However, as you try to promote your work, it feels like you're spitting words into the wind.

Your promotional messages, like autumn leaves, drift into the street with a thousand others only to land in an anonymous pile, soon to be swept away into forgetfulness.

You're just another tree shedding leaves into the marketplace. Or, to change the metaphor, you're one more radio station along an infinite dial of voices and static—and your listeners are continuously scanning.

For decades, I've known the discouragement of doing absolutely brilliant (and pretty awful) marketing, and then seeing virtually no response. It's enough to drive you batty. If you know what I'm saying, you're not alone.

Welcome the reality of business (and life) where we are drowned out daily. Where even the best companies are constantly up against the greatest challenge of all—minds inundated by endless stuff.

Your greatest competition is not your competition. It's the NOISE.

We think our greatest competition is company X or Y, and we tailor our messages to counter them. But those competitors are in the same boat you are—like Sisyphus, constantly pushing the boulder uphill against the noise.

We end up having to spend a huge amount of our time and effort trying to get somebody to listen. Trying to get the attention of our potential clients. Trying to stand out in a swirl of noise and distraction. It's a daunting task, and a challenge that we all face in business.

Even as you read this chapter, you're being distracted—right?

We can't change our noisy world or our crowded marketplace. But we can learn to send a clear, compelling, memorable signal that rises above the static. We can, with the help of some brain science and some thoughtful word-crafting, break through the barriers that prevent our message from taking hold.

We can meet this challenge with the greatest competitive advantage of all—**Clarity**.

Companies grow to a certain point based on effort, luck, and devoted early customers who help us get started. But many businesses stall because they don't craft a clear direction and clear messages that stand out in a noisy marketplace.

Sometimes we think our customers are dense because we've already told them what we do and why we're great more than twenty-five times. But, in fact, they're not dense—they're distracted. You are one of a thousand voices each day.

We begin to question our value proposition and think that we should cast a wider net to appeal to a greater number of people.

That's a huge mistake.

What we have to do is learn how to compete with the noise, and that is where some brain science will provide the crucial keys to success.

How does the human brain cope with the vast array of impressions it receives every day— thousands of advertisements, hundreds of messages, the babble of external voices, internal thoughts and feelings? With screens everywhere and quiet nowhere, why is it that we don't melt down into quivering masses of over-stimulated paralysis?

Enter the *Reticular Activating System*, or RAS for short.

This marvelous part of your brain exists not only to regulate your sleep/wake cycle but also to serve as your primary filter, bringing to your attention what is most crucial and blurring the rest into the background. It's the gatekeeper between sensory information and your conscious mind.

Without the RAS, we'd each descend into overloaded madness. The RAS allows us to function in a world full of noise and distraction because it is on the lookout for what is:

- Relevant
- New
- Important
- Entertaining

All the rest is kept at bay by this marvelous control system. Survival dictates that our brains filter out the tsunami of noise so we can focus in on what matters.

Thank God for the RAS! It is a great blessing, but it is also your biggest challenge. Unless your message is relevant, new, important, and/or entertaining, guess what it is? That's right—noise. You are one of a thousand distractions on any given day.

So many messages never hit their mark because they don't have clarity. They aren't focused, relevant, and memorable. They aren't quickly and easily understood by a mind with a lot of other things on its agenda.

About ten years ago, I remember consulting with a small digital advertising agency about their messaging. I analyzed their website and other materials and explained that they came across as JADA—Just Another Digital Agency. Same offerings, same buzzwords, same promises. Yawn.

Now, in fact, they did have some differentiation, but nobody could find it by looking at their materials. I believe most companies have differentiators which need to be brought to the surface and expressed clearly. However, the majority of websites I look at suffer from Just Another Syndrome.

But here's the wonderful flipside—if you can differentiate, if you know how to get through the filter, you then stand out from the competition. You rise above the noise.

Knowing that every person in your audience has this internal gatekeeper is the key to promotional success. You don't necessarily have to be the biggest, the best, or the only. But you can become the **clearest**. Your hurdle isn't all those other companies out there. It's the RAS.

The brain isn't impressed with Just Another _____. The RAS is keenly attuned to WWIFM—What's In It For Me. And if your message doesn't get to that point quickly, you're tuned out.

People are busy. The RAS is active. You only have a few seconds to make an impact. You're either clear and interesting, or you're forgotten.

So, what does it mean to have clarity? Let's look at five crucial elements to business clarity that can help any company gain greater success through razor-sharp focus and effective go-to-market messaging:

- **Clear Direction**

- **Clear Offering**

- **Clear Bulls-eye Customer**

- **Clear Value**

- **Memorable Messaging**

Clear Direction

The first, and most crucial, element of business clarity is having a well-thought-out direction. You can't move from Point A to Point B unless you have a clear destination (Point B) in mind. The first step in your roadmap, or your business GPS, is setting the direction.

It's important to note here that directions and goals do change. Often, a company will start out with a certain offering or clientele, and then there is some morphing along the way. That is to be expected, but new direction evolves by setting the compass and moving forward. Spinning around in indecision is a sure way to become undifferentiated—just another entity waiting for others to tell it what to do (which is like walking around in a Will Work for Food sign).

Here are the questions I typically ask business owners who are trying to settle on their long-term direction:

- Why did you start this company in the first place?
- What are the boundaries (domain, vertical, industry, etc.) of your niche?
- What unmet needs are current and potential clients truly looking for in this niche?
- What do you want this company to become (and not become)?
- What work have you done so far that clients have raved about?

- What work have you done so far that has been unfulfilling or a failure?
- What larger currents and waves—trends, and growth, and shrinkage—are shaping the niche you occupy (or want to occupy)?

The key point here is that no company can be everything to everyone. Many businesses hesitate to come to a more defined direction because they don't want to turn down any opportunity, but it is that very mindset that sinks all efforts at clarity. Many opportunities are the wrong opportunities for your company. It is up to you to define your sweet spot.

In general, you want to pursue a business direction where the tide is already coming in and where market conditions are pointing to current need and future growth. Being in a shrinking marketplace, or a crowded niche where companies and their offerings are viewed as commodities, is choosing to push the boulder uphill.

I have often counseled companies to narrow their direction dramatically in order to avoid being Just Another Provider. In fact, I worked for ten years in one company that had a tremendous niche offering but also tried to expand into a crowded space with plenty of competition. We could not differentiate in that very tempting, adjacent market space. It was an expensive lesson.

One phrase I use often is, "Not all business is good business." By proactively deciding in which direction good sweet-spot business is likely to be found, you dramatically increase your chances of long-term success.

So we map out where we want to go, but exactly how are we helping our clients.

Clear Offering

What does an electrician offer for services? Seems pretty clear, right?

How about a business productivity consultant?

What about a company that says it provides IT and technical solutions?

The fact is, many business use terms that don't have a self-evident meaning to the marketplace. I know precisely when to refer a trusted electrician, but unless I know exactly what a business productivity consultant does, for whom, and what the customer pain point is, I have no idea if I need them.

And I have no idea how to refer them to others.

We assume that we understand what it is we offer to the marketplace, but until we step out of our own shoes, we may not realize that we're not communicating effectively to the outside world. We have all this information in our heads, and we assume that our audience also gets it. Trust me; they probably don't. I've had customers who've met me multiple times, received tons of emails from me over years, and then they'll ask me, "Tell me, what exactly is it that you do again?"

Sometimes I ask people in my industry to explain what I do to someone else. This is always a telling moment as to whether my message has gotten across (and lots of times, it hasn't).

The shipping company UPS manages to fail to communicate with frightening regularity. Quick—what is the five-word phrase that now occupies space on their massive fleet of trucks, viewed by millions of everyday people, every day?

"*Synchronizing the world of commerce.*" They're trying to take their message about supply chain logistics and communicate it broadly without considering that only 0.01% of the population cares about, or understands, this aspect of their offering.

Everyday people don't buy commerce synchronization.

Your offering must make sense to your audience—both your potential customers, AND those who might refer you to others. Your message needs to be very clear and simple. Nobody has time to help you figure out your business. It's your job to communicate your offering to everyday people who have their minds stuffed with a bunch of other important matters.

Packaging your offering involves answering questions, such as:

- Is what I do a one-time thing, or an ongoing service?
- Is there any intellectual property that I am licensing (instead of a product or service that is a purchase-to-own transaction)?
- How will customers pay for this (capital budget, operating expense, other)?
- What is the repeat or add-on business potential, if any (hint: you want any!)
- What makes my offering different from others that are available?
- What makes my company different as a provider? (put another way – what's my value-add?)

- What success story can I tell about a satisfied client?

What you want to do, as much as possible, is "*thing-ify*" your offering—package it up so that people can easily wrap their minds around it and envision exchanging dollars for it. If people don't understand it, they won't pay for it. And that's why we have to strip down the jargon and make our product or service very plain.

One of my favorite consultant websites—now no longer on-line—was absolutely masterful at spinning a web of incomprehensible jargon, so that no-one could possibly understand what was being offered. Here is a sample:

We have pioneered a new model for sustainable, consumer-driven growth based on principles of complex adaptive systems. This is a new premise for strategy for a world undergoing deep structural change: different assumptions about creating value, different path to market and business development, a different frame of reference to see and think. Ecosystems are the new basis of competition. The companies that know how to position and manage themselves as platforms for self-organization can make Google-like growth almost template driven.

HUH?? The entire website was loaded with this kind of gibberish. It was one of the largest tsunamis of buzzword noise ever witnessed by man or beast.

At the most, we have a few seconds to make an impression and explain what we do. That's true on the web, at trade shows, on phone calls, and in sales presentations. Nobody has the time or bandwidth to translate our jargon into real-world clarity. We need to make our offering clear if we want wallets to open.

Clarity is all about getting the right message to the right people about why we're the right fit for them. Our offering is our "fit", but who are the right people?

Clear Bulls-eye Customer

Not everyone is your customer. You cannot service seven billion people. You have to narrow your focus. I don't know about you, but I can only handle a tiny sliver of the human population. That's true of every company, even in the Fortune 100.

We often hear about a target market or customer, but I like to get even more precise—defining our bulls-eye customer. I don't want you to refer me to a generalized group. We want referrals to those specific people ready to pay for what we do, right?

Your bulls-eye customer is the one with the pain you can fix and the budget to pay you to fix it. That's a smaller group than you may think, especially that last part, regarding money.

Needs are everywhere, but unless you plan to be a charity, you have to define who are the potential customers that have budget dollars and painful business challenges in your sweet spot.

I have a friend who works with a company that provides managed IT services for larger churches and other non-profits. Now, I know there are potentially a million companies in a thousand verticals that might need managed IT services, but they have chosen their niche based on specific expertise, track record, interest, and contacts.

And they know the size of customer that requires their services with the commensurate budget to pay for them. That's how a relatively small company can dominate in a tightly-defined niche. By painting an accurate portrait of the ideal client, that's how solid referrals can be activated.

Ask yourself these questions:

- What type of company/ organization/ person/ entity do I help?
- What is the vertical (industry) or horizontal (functional area, e.g. HR, or Marketing) where my customers reside?
- What size of entity needs my services, and has the budget?
- What is/are the title(s)/roles of those who make decisions for what I do?
- What specific business challenge(s) plague them right now?
- How would I describe the customers I don't want?
- Who are the people most likely connected to my bulls-eye customers?

The fact is, every person you encounter will pigeonhole you/your company because, if you're lucky, you may get only one pixel of space in their memory. So why not describe that pigeonhole clearly—including your bulls-eye customer—so that they can do business with you or refer you accurately?

Now that you've described your ideal clientele, you have to explain why you have something unique that will help them.

Clear Value

It's time to discuss the D-word – *Differentiation*.

Why should I do business with your company? What makes your offering different/better? What's your "secret sauce," or "magic superpower"?

If you're not differentiated, you're noise. You're a commodity. You're Just Another _____. Remember, the RAS is looking for new and different. Relevant. Not the same-old song and dance.

Some products or services are differentiated simply because they're.... well, so different. Tesla automobiles. Amazon. Printing paper. OK, maybe not printing paper...

But what about lawyers? Training companies? PR agencies? Printing/packaging companies? Desk chairs?

I haven't consulted with any desk chairs, but I have worked with other types of providers and, in each case, there is a differentiator hiding in the closet, waiting to be brought out and polished off. Sometimes it's in the method, other times in the experience, and sometimes it's all about the personality. The value to the customer that matters can be best expressed this way: *pain relief.*

- What is the business problem that needs to be solved?

- How does the customer feel about this issue? (emotions lead to action)
- What are the obvious and hidden business costs being experienced by the customer?
- How do we uniquely diagnose or treat the business disorder?
- Why are we trustworthy and competent compared to others?
- How does investment in my company look small compared to the resulting growth and/or savings?
- How will the customer feel after the upcoming "fix" of the problem?
- How do I explain the value we've provided to a similar customer?

If it's not a felt pain, it won't be acted on. That's why it's important to explain the value, not just in abstract or logical terms, but in emotional and personal language. People want to stay compliant, save face, keep their jobs, get rid of a time sink, get promoted, grow revenue, impress their peers, and accomplish more….making these things happen for them is what you're actually offering. Pain relief.

Fix the headache. Fulfill the yearning. Show how progress is possible (with your help, of course).

As part of my consulting practice, I come in as an outside resource and help companies reach clarity (because…you can't read the label of the jar you're in.) That's my differentiation. Yet, at times, I have also been "stuck" in confusion like my clients, because I cannot see my own business objectively. I've had to turn to others to help me fix that very real business pain. The King of Clarity also needs clarity!

Now we turn to this: how do we package your clear direction, clear offering, clear bulls-eye, and clear value in such a way that people get it in as few words as possible?

Memorable Messaging

I have seen so much atrocious messaging that I'm afraid some of my brain cells suffer from PTSD. If you wanted to repel potential customers and leave them in a fog, you couldn't do much better than to use such language as:

We leverage scalable enterprise-wide collaboration solutions to enable customer-centric next-level executive bloviation across multiple silos of technological bamboozlement.

Exactly who is going to refer your company, and to whom? For what? Why?

Long-winded explanations are noise. Nobody has time to process all of that.

Let's go back to our previous point about having one pixel of memory in the minds of your audience. And remember that we have to get through the RAS filter with very clear, simple, relevant language. How do we do this?

I encourage companies to develop several memory darts, not an elevator speech. These are quick-hit, compact word packages that are designed to cut through the noise, make the right point, and stick in memory.

I like to develop four interrelated memory darts:

1.   The   single-sentence   summary: I/We _____ (fix this business pain) _____ for _____ (bulls-eye customer) _____ by _____ (differentiating superpower) _____.

2. The memory-hook analogy: We are like the _____ of _____.

3. The company narrative: We came to be doing this by growing through this evolutionary process _____.

4. The relevant success story: I was working with a client last week who was experiencing

_____, and so we
_____.

The reason these memory darts work is because they are not sterile factoids—they are real-life and contain personality and emotion. Human beings respond to (and remember) stories, and we find it far easier to grasp something if it can be hooked onto something else pre-existing in our minds (which is why an analogy is so powerful).

Let me give an example. My clarity consulting business grew out of another entrepreneurial endeavor (called Impactiviti) in which I "match-make" pharma training departments with targeted, optimal outsource vendors. It's a bit of a non-standard business model—a hybrid of a broker, headhunter, consultant, and referral agent—which means I have to explain it to customers with memory darts like this:

1. Impactiviti helps simplify the bewildering world of selecting outsource vendors by discussing your training needs with you, then identifying the best vendors from my hand-selected network of 60+ providers. *(single-sentence summary)*
2. Think of me as the eHarmony of pharmaceutical training. *(analogy)*
3. Having worked on the vendor side for ten years, I kept seeing this nagging problem—

my clients did not know who the best vendors were for a given project, and the vendors often didn't differentiate themselves effectively. As a trusted intermediary, I figured I could fix both of those issues by making intelligent referrals in a win-win business model. *(Impactiviti company narrative)*

4. Just last week, I helped _____ Pharmaceuticals, who was looking for a provider of on-line Managed Markets training modules. They didn't know where to turn, but after 5 minutes of discussion, I knew exactly which company to connect them with. *(success story)*

When meeting with a new potential client or explaining your business to a possible referral partner, these compact, high-impact memory darts allow you to accurately get your point across in a memorable fashion. Rather than a blizzard of bullet points or a jargon-filled overview of concepts (both of which will be lost in the noise), these core messages dramatically increase your chances of being quickly understood, and getting retained in memory.

Any and every business needs a verbal business card to spark understanding and ignite more referrals. That's what memory darts are for. Imagine how much more effective networking meetings are when you're not merely exchanging paper business cards; instead, you're getting a clear message across the RAS and into memory.

So, here's the reality: we all have the same competition—the noise. Our audiences have limited memory capacity, limited processing bandwidth, and short attention spans, which means that one of our primary tasks is shaping our message to rise above the noise and find the bulls-eye. *This makes clarity our secret weapon and our key competitive advantage*.

We want to be so clear and memorable that people can pass on the essence of our business to others, much like passing a baton in a relay race. Clarity is what makes us referral-ready, and we all know that referrals are the most effective way to power a business forward. If you're looking to grow your business beyond its current level, your first step should be...well, backwards. Take a step back and make sure YOU are clear about where you're going and who you're helping, then find the right words to make this message crystal clear to others.

Every day without clarity means another day of lost opportunity. Out of all the challenges you face, being Just Another _____ in a sea of static is one problem you can definitely fix. Let other companies stay lost in the noise while you send out a clear signal!

Steve Woodruff

Steve Woodruff has worked in sales, marketing, and consulting for over thirty years with clients ranging from Fortune 50 pharmaceutical companies, to SMBs, to solo consultants. He is known as the King of Clarity because of his unique ability to analyze and assess any company's position and messaging and help figure out their "fit" in the marketplace. Steve is also an avid builder of business referral networks in the life sciences vertical as well as in his hometown Nashville area.

He is the father of five young men, the caretaker of one dog and two cats, and the unending life project of his very patient wife, Sandy.

Steve drinks far too much coffee and actively blogs on business themes at SteveWoodruff.com

2

Personal Branding:
How to Build an Army of Buyers Who
Know, Like, and Trust You Before
They've Even Ever Met You

Here's the Big Problem

The world changed.

You had your nose to the grindstone, making stuff happen, getting deals done, building a business the best way you knew how, through hard work, common sense, and a lot of the time, sheer force of will.

It got you this far. But the world changed.

And the things that you got you this far are not going be the same things that get you to the next level. The things that got you this far aren't even going to keep you treading water.

Whatever business you're in, the primary purpose of your business is creating and maintaining customers. At the end of the day, as the chief cook and bottle washer, your primary job function is creating and maintaining customers.

Maybe you're not cold calling anymore. Maybe you don't sit in on the pitches. So maybe you haven't noticed the big change.

It's not so much that customers have changed. People are people. Human wants, needs, and desires have been fairly consistent for the last ten thousand years or so.

But the way we go about satisfying those wants, needs, and desires has shifted dramatically in the last ten years. I can even tell you the exact date the world changed:

January 9, 2007.

That was the day Steve Jobs introduced the iPhone to the world.

Just a few months earlier, Mark Zuckerberg opened Facebook up to anyone in the world with a valid email address. Before then, only the cool kids were allowed at the table.

The unique combination of having fingertip access to both the sum total of all human knowledge and a rapidly expanding network of "friends" from around the globe fundamentally changed human interaction.

If you don't believe me, go sit in a room with a few teenagers for any length of time.

It's not just kids; it's not just hipsters and millennials. Communication has changed for everyone, and it has changed the way customers interact with companies like yours.

Ten years ago, the sales funnel looked pretty much the same as it had since the dawn of trade. If you were a silk merchant in a bazaar, you would set up your stand with your finest, brightest, most colorful cloth prominently displayed, blowing in the wind, and you would stand nearby doing whatever it took to engage passersby in a conversation.

Once you had them talking, you had all the power. They didn't know the first thing about thread count, or exotic dyes, or the seven brave camels who gave their lives to bring your silk across the Himalayas from the farthest reaches of the orient.

They sure didn't know how much silk like yours cost anywhere else. They probably didn't know anywhere else they could even buy silk like yours.

Because they were already talking to you, you had the power.

After that, it was just a numbers game. If you got 100 people a day to engage in a conversation, fifty of them would ask the right questions you clearly knew were buying signals, you'd end up shaking hands, and closing deals with twenty of them. Voila... the world's first sales funnel.

Attention. Interest. Desire. Action.

Our silk merchant only had to get their attention to keep the sales funnel full. And ten years ago, that's really all you had to do. Get them a brochure. Get them in. Get them talking.

But you don't have a monopoly on the information now. And the power dynamic between buyers and sellers has been irrevocably altered.

Today's silk buyers have access to the sum total of all human knowledge about the silk trade at their fingertips. They can find a hundred other vendors selling similar fabrics. They can research your competition. They can research your prices. They can research your quality. They can research your reputation.

And they can do all of that without ever bothering to put on pants and leave the house, much less contact you to get the information. The sales funnel is broken because they only need you for the final step: ACTION.

The sad truth is this—in today's instant access economy, if you're not on their shopping list before they start shopping, you don't stand a chance.

A Little Too Ironic. Yeah, I Really Do Think.

It would almost be funny if your family's livelihood and the future of your business didn't hang in the balance. The ironic part is that even though so much of the sales process happens online before you get a chance to influence the customer's decisions, before you get a chance to tell your story, before you start building a relationship with the potential buyer, people are still people, and people still prefer to do business with people they know, like, and trust.

But you don't get a chance to help them know, like, and trust you until they've already reached the bottom of the sales funnel, after they've researched their purchase, after they've made all the important decisions, and after they've decided how much they're willing to pay. Your product is turned into a commodity and the only thing you can do is smile and hope they like you.

I work with a lot of people in the automotive retail business. Over ninety percent of all vehicle purchases begin with an online search. But according to the National Automobile Dealers Association, over seventy percent of people who buy a new vehicle bought the car they bought because they liked and trusted their salesperson.

People prefer to do business with people they know, like, and trust.

Your customers don't need you for access to information anymore. Information is everywhere.

But they still need you for confirmation, to assure them that they actually understand what they think they understand. They need you for customization, to help them see how the generic information they've found fits into their actual life and makes it better. And they need you for personalization—the human touch—to hold their hand, look them in the eye, and let them know they are making the right decision, that everything is going to be okay.

So, you've got a choice. You can wait for them at the finish line, pounce on them once they've decided on a course of action, and hope you can magically gain their friendship and trust in the brief time you have before they decide on a different course of action.

Or you can meet them at the starting gate and run the race with them, showering them with useful, helpful information, guiding their decision-making process without trying to sell them anything; simply being a friend until the time comes for them to be a customer.

If you're in business, you're in sales. And if you're in sales, you're in the business of making friends.

That's the way it's always been. That's why the ad execs on Mad Men had three-martini lunches with clients every day. That's the reason half the people on the golf course ever picked up a club. That's why we sit through horrible, overcooked chicken lunches every week at the Rotary Club.

Making friends gets deals done.

But the world changed.

And you've got the greatest tool in the history of the universe—in your pocket, on your desk, or possibly in your hand right now—for making friends, for forming human bonds and connections, for building an army of people who know, like, and trust you before they've ever even met you... your smartphone.

Your network is your net worth. But your network isn't limited to people that you meet in the Rotary club or on the golf course. Today, you can build a worldwide network connecting with people in every corner of the world.

Opportunities arise from connections.

When you first started in business, you were probably told you would never get a second chance to make a first impression, that you had to dress for success. That perception was reality.

Who you were was determined in large part by the clothes you wore, the way you carried yourself, and the strength of your handshake. In today's world, odds are pretty good that your first impression won't happen at the Rotary Club. Today, first impressions happen online, on social media, or on Google.

We research everything online from things we buy to people we meet. We research our babysitters, our dog walkers, and you better best believe, your customers will be Googling your company, your sales people, and yes, they'll be Googling you.

You are who Google says you are.

If Google doesn't say anything at all about you, that's bad. And if Google is saying the wrong things about you, that's worse.

The front page of Google's search results for your name is a pretty good indication of who the world thinks you are, what you can do, and what you're about.

That's really all your personal brand is:

The Idea of You That Exists in the Minds of Others

Your personal brand is simply a fancy, schmancy word for your reputation.

Dale Carnegie said that eighty-five percent of your success in any endeavor depends not on your know-how or technical skill but on your people skills and your ability to communicate, convince, and convert. Back in the day, you were told that it wasn't what you know, it's who you know.

But that was then.

The communication revolution of the last decade has turned that old saw on its head too. Your success is still dependent on your ability to communicate, convince, and convert. But with the collapse of the sales funnel, it's not who you know, it's who knows you.

And they need to know you before they need you.

If you're not on their shopping list before they start shopping, you're out of luck.

Your reputation precedes you. It always has. The difference now is that the entire world has your reputation at their fingertips... unless they can't find you and, in that case, your conspicuous absence says everything they need to know about your reputation.

Humans are social creatures. We hunt in packs.

We go where the herd leads us.

A well-defined, highly visible, overwhelmingly positive personal brand lets your new friends and potential buyers know that the herd approves and that you're the kind of person they can do business with. If other people know, like, and trust you, and if Google and Facebook appear to know, like, and trust you, that provides social cues to lower their defenses and think that maybe, just maybe, they should know, like, and trust you too.

The gurus call it social proof. That's the endgame—generating enough social proof to deserve a spot on the shopping list.

The question is how?

The answer is by using the right words and pictures.

The big mistake most folks make when they set out to build their personal brand is trying to build a personal brand. So here's the first rule of personal branding: don't talk about personal branding.

It ain't about you.

Your reputation, your personal brand, is the idea of you that exists in the minds of others. If you spend all day on Facebook, and Twitter, and MySpace posting selfies and talking about how great you are, how talented you are, how successful you are, then the only idea that's going to exist in other people's minds is that you are a narcissistic, egotistical, self-centered jerkwad.

You see a lot of self-proclaimed experts, gurus, ninjas, and rockstars on social media and you can probably be sure that they're not.

You want the idea organically forming in people's heads that you are competent and helpful, that you have the skill set to solve their problems, and the mindset to make their lives better.

If that's the flower you want to bloom, you need to plant the right seed:

The Micro Manifesto

Instead of telling people how great you are, tell people how helpful you are, who you can help, and how you can help them.

The Micro Manifesto is the elevator speech for an online world in which we no longer meet each other in elevators.

You've got a minute or two between the garage and the thirty-first floor to tell the story of you. In today's online world, you only have seconds before they click to the next page, swipe to the next profile, or scroll to the next grumpy cat in their timeline.

To be exact, you have twenty to twenty-five words to plant the seed that will grow into the idea of YOU. That's how many words you're going to able to fit in your social media intro/bio/headline sections and that's how many words Google is going to grab from your website and your profiles to put into search engine results.

When people Google your name or stalk you on Facebook, they're only going to see twenty to twenty-five words. You'd better make them count.

The formula for building the most effective Micro Manifesto is fill-in-the-blank simple. In twenty-five words or less, state the following:

I help (WHO)_____ (do WHAT)_____.

Here's mine:

I help salespeople and entrepreneurs build an army of buyers who know, like, and trust you before they've ever even met you.

I help (WHO - salespeople and entrepreneurs) (do WHAT - build an army of buyers who know, like, and trust you before they've ever even met you.)

If you search for me on Google, Google is going to tell you exactly that, in exactly those words, five or six times on the front page of the results because that's exactly what I want you to hear and that's exactly what I've trained Google to tell you. That's the seed I've planted.

They say a picture is worth a thousand words.
I think that's a little on the low side, especially if you're using the right picture.

Your social media profile pic is your de facto stand-in in the online, virtual world. For all intents and purposes, and as far as people who have never met you are concerned, IT IS YOU. It's the image in their head when they think of you, when they interact with you online, and when they read your recent postings.

That image in their mind is much more powerful than you've ever imagined.

There's growing evidence detailed in articles from the journal Science, Scientific American, and others that facial images are determining factors in a variety of human interactions ranging from how long judges will sentence convicts to prison to which candidates voters will put in the White House.

One study shows that children as young as five years old can predict, with an amazing degree of accuracy, the outcome of an election simply by choosing which candidate "looks" more competent in a photo.

There are entire regions of the brain dedicated to recognizing faces and making snap judgments about them. Friend or foe? Is that a warm, fuzzy kitten face or a hungry, lion face? These lasting impressions are formed within a tenth of a second, long before we've had time to read the words near the picture.

First impressions are visual, and you never get a second chance to make a first impression.

Your profile pic will, in large part, determine whether people like and trust you.

Here are six keys to likable, trustworthy profile pics:

1. **Use a pic of you and only you**. Not your logo. Not your car. Not your dog. Not you and your dog. Not you and your spouse, your kids, or that random celebrity you met that one time. And please, please, please not you and two-thirds of an arm and one eyeball of whoever it is that you cropped out of a picture from last year's office Christmas party because you liked the dress you were wearing. You and only you.

2. **Use a face shot.** Sure every professional photographer and wannabe actor in Hollywood calls them headshots. But it's not about your head. It's called Facebook for a reason.

3. **Make eye contact.** It's the first thing they teach you in Sales 101. People don't trust you if you can't look them in the eye. It works in the real world. And it works online.

4. **Get the lighting right.** You don't want shadows on your face and you don't want lights so bright they make you squint. Nobody likes a squinter. Paying a professional photographer will be the best hundred bucks you've ever spent, but if you're not ready for that, just step outside, away from the fluorescent lights, on a nice partly sunny day. Keep the sun in front of you. Easy Peasy.

5. **Stay away from cluttered backgrounds.** A clear blue sky makes a great background. Or a blank wall. Those are your options. The only thing you want people making snap judgments about is you, not the leftover pizza on the desk behind you.

6. **Smile.** You've told your people a thousand times to answer the phone with a smile. Smiling at others makes them smile, it makes them happy, and it makes them like you whether they want to or not. And please, for the love of everything you hold dear… no duck lips!

You'll have plenty of opportunities to display your unique personality, this isn't one of them. Get one good, simple, boring headshot and use it across all your social media profiles. One consistent image of you for people to see wherever they find you.

As Ye Sow, So Shall Ye Reap

There you have it. The seeds you need to plant that will blossom into the desired idea of you in the minds of your customers. The words and pictures necessary to form the mental image of you as both competent and helpful.

Unfortunately, you can't just start cracking people's skulls open and tilling away. You must spread the seeds far and wide, more like a tree raining pollen in the wind than a farmer hoeing a row.

And, you must train the search engines and social media platforms to the tell the story you want to be told and to spread your seeds for you.

You train Google and you train Facebook to use the right words and images the same way you train a new puppy to fetch—reward and repetition, only Google and Facebook aren't interested in Scooby Snacks and Doggie Biscuits. There's only one thing that you can do to make Google and Facebook pay attention to you:

Create more content.

Search engines and social media platforms are content consuming machines. They eat content for breakfast, lunch, and dinner. They exist with the sole purpose of gathering words, pictures, and video, chewing them up and spitting them out, running them through their algorithms, recycling, repurposing, and reusing them, finding new audiences, attracting new eyeballs, and making a few pennies selling access to those new eyeballs.

300 million pictures a day are uploaded to Facebook.
500 hours of video is uploaded to YouTube every minute.

Every single second 6,000 tweets are tweeted and 40,000 searches are performed on Google.
And yet, the monsters are still hungry and willing to do your bidding if you feed them.

For a quarter of a century, Dan Rather was one of the most powerful voices in America. From behind the anchor desk at the CBS Evening News, he reached millions of viewers shaping public opinion, influencing national policy, and creating conversations around countless dinner tables.

Back then, it took one of the largest media conglomerates in the history of the world and a nationwide network of local affiliate stations to make all that possible.

In 2016, he did it sitting at home in his underwear, playing around on Facebook.

After Donald Trump hinted that Second Amendment supporters could solve his Hillary problem with a bullet, Dan rather published a brief post on his Facebook page and quickly reached twenty million readers.

He rarely, if ever, pulled in those kinds of numbers at CBS. And these days, CBS is lucky to reach six million folks a night.

The media landscape hasn't changed; it's been decimated and built again from the ground up.

The average viewership of the big three evening newscasts is down sixty percent from its peak. Most people now get their news from social media.

That's bad news for the TV networks and it's even worse news for newspapers. The media titans and conglomerates are still trying to figure out the economics of the new digital world.

But the bad news for them is great news for Dan Rather.

And it's great news for you and your business.

> *"I've gone through the print era, the radio era, the television era," says Rather in an interview with The Atlantic. "I've become totally, completely convinced that the potential here is to reach a truly mass audience—and, by the way, a mass international audience. Facebook and its offsprings are the future."*

You don't need a nationwide network of TV stations and millions of dollars in equipment to tell your story now. That same magic device you have in your pocket that connects you to a worldwide network of potential customers has a high definition video camera built-in that's better than all the giant broadcast cameras that Dan Rather ever stared into.

You don't have to be Dan Rather to step in front of the camera. You don't have to be Steven Spielberg to create a video. You don't have to be William Shakespeare to create a blog post. And you don't need to be Paul Harvey to start a podcast and tell the rest of the story.

You have all the tools and technology. All you need is a story to tell and the willingness to put yourself out there.

Zig Ziglar said that bashful salespeople have skinny children. That's never been more true than it is today. If you're not creating content, entertaining, informing, or vying for attention, your voice will never be heard in today's noisy world.

But what should you create?

The first and most important content you need to be creating doesn't even come from you. It comes from your customers.

Reviews, endorsements, and testimonials are the ultimate social proof.

You can scream all day long about how great you are, but everyone will take that with a grain of salt. Get a handful of other people to start saying how great you and your company are, get Google, Facebook, and LinkedIn to start spreading the word and your buyers will believe it.

You are who Google says you are.

Reviews are worth their weight in gold, but you have to work for them. You have to deliver what you promise to earn them. You have to ask your customers to write them (begging and bribing shouldn't be ruled out). And you have to make it easy and painless for your customers to say nice things about you.

After you get some reviews, start creating your own content. Shower your network with helpful content that answers their questions, informs them about your product and your industry, and solves their problems.

And you should do all of that without trying to sell them anything.

Just like at the Rotary Club, nobody wants to talk to the guy who wades into the crowd with a fistful of business cards and starts trying to sell you his great new weight loss/multivitamin/home income opportunity before the wilted lettuce is even on the table.

Give it away until it hurts. The whole idea is to present yourself as both competent and helpful.
But every once in a while, you've got to ask for the order.

In his book, *Jab Jab Jab, Right Hook,* social media consultant Gary Vaynerchuk compares social media to a heavyweight title boxing match.

Feel your audience out and soften them up with helpful, informative, entertaining content and postings:

☐ Here's a blog post about how to save money when you're buying a new computer system for the office - JAB!

☐ Here's a video about ways to streamline your hiring process - JAB

☐ Here's our latest podcast about recent IRS changes and how they affect your bottom line - JAB!

Then, after you've established yourself as competent and helpful, you throw the haymaker, the big right hook!

If you're not asking for the order, if you're not reaching out to your audience by phone, email, or through social advertising, and if you're not trying to get deals done, then you might as well post cat videos.

Right now, you have at your fingertips everything you need to make new friends around the world. I'm talking about my favorite kind of friends—friends with benefits—the benefit being that every once in a while, they give you money!

The Story You Tell the World Changes Your World

Up until a few years ago, I tried to keep my private life private. I was flying under the radar and that's the way I liked it. Then I had a good customer change jobs. Once he got settled into his new company, he wanted me to do some work for him but he couldn't remember the name of my company; he only remembered my name. And he couldn't find me on the internet.

He told me all of that three years later when we finally reconnected.

That was the day I started making sure that if someone wanted to give Terry Lancaster a check, they'd better be able to find me. That Google, Facebook, and all of the rest of them were telling the story I wanted to be told.

I registered the domain TerryLancaster.com, started blogging, and started connecting with customers on social media.

I developed deeper, more meaningful relationships with my customers because we talked more often and we had something to talk about besides business. We became friends.

The blogging lead to writing in industry publications and speeches at industry events. My customers started reaching out to me to solve bigger problems. And when you solve bigger problems, you get bigger checks.

More money is great, but something else happened too. Executive headhunters started reaching out to me. Venture capitalists started calling. People began to see me in a whole new light.

Every step along the way people were willing to listen to what I had to say because more and more it looked like I knew what I was talking about.

And perception is reality.

The story you tell the world changes your world.

It changes the way your customers look at you.

It changes the way your employees look at you.

And the right story will change the way you look at yourself.

George Bernard Shaw said that life isn't about finding yourself. Life is about creating yourself.

As you set off on this journey of self-creation, remember this one thing: Never try to be something you're not. It's not about puffing yourself up. It's not about you at all. It's about who you can help and how you can help them.

People can smell a phony from a mile away. They can smell it at the Rotary Club and they can smell it online.

In the immortal words of Tyler Durden, sticking feathers up your butt doesn't make you a chicken.

Never try to be something you're not.

But never be afraid to be more of who you truly are.

———

Terry Lancaster

I help salespeople and entrepreneurs build an army of buyers who know, like, and trust you before they've ever even met you.

Over the last three decades, I've worked with thousands of successful businesses offering proven strategies for making the cash register ring.
I can help you build your personal brand, find your authentic voice, and tell your story to the world because the story you tell the world changes your world.

My book *BETTER! Self-Help For The Rest Of Us* is an Amazon #1 Best Seller with glowing reviews from around the world thanking me for the understandable, actionable, life-changing ideas and stories. I am a contributing writer for

Forbes, The Good Men Project, and *Dealer Marketing.*

I have spoken to audiences from coast to coast at TEDx, The National Association of Broadcasters, and the National Automobile Dealers Association. I only take the stage to do two things—change lives and chew gum. And I'm all out of gum.

Born and raised in Nashville, TN, I have a degree in English/Journalism from Tennessee Technological University where I learned how to program ginormous room-sized computers using a deck of cards and a rubber band, and how to edit newspaper and radio ads using a ruler, a razor blade, and scotch tape. While all of that may make me sound MacGyver cool, it hasn't come in handy much since graduation.

Mary, my wife of thirty years, and I are the proud parents of three daughters and I spend most of my time, like every other middle-aged, overweight, native southerner, at the ice rink playing hockey.

Find out more and connect with me on TerryLancaster.com

3

The Online Sales Mistake Most Businesses Make (and What to Do About It)

I'm Juliana Stachurski. I'm a mother of eight kids (yes same father, yes we're married, yes we're Catholic) who understands "multiple hats" is really just code for you're going to have to do it all.

I've been in business since I was five years old. I begged my parents to let me run a lemonade stand so that I could earn my own money and they obliged. Ever the banker, my father informed me that if I wanted to have a business, I was going to have to pay for my supplies. They charged me for the lemonade concentrate and cups. (They let me use the pitcher, water, small table and access to the street without charge because, you know, I was family).

I charged ten cents a cup. My parents made sure I knew how to count change and I dutifully made my sign out of crayon on the inside of a cereal box. I was SO EXCITED when I made sales that day! I was especially proud that Sunday when the basket came by my pew and I could put in money that I had EARNED into the basket. And I DID! I put all $3 in the basket.

And then I cried.

Because nobody told me that the guy with the basket at church doesn't give change.

There have been many more times I have cried since that day because of the consequence of what I didn't know. Unlike when I was five, I don't have a rich uncle to give me $3 and bail me out of my ignorance. If you don't have a rich uncle to erase your mistakes and you want to learn how to leverage your way out of being stuck, the systems and strategies in this book will help your business break through to the next level.

Since my foray into lemonade sales, I've had the privilege of working with an opera company, multi-national hotel brands, small brick-and-mortar businesses, and online companies. Most recently, I had a chance to work with a celebrity brand and play an instrumental role in driving massive growth using online marketing.

Here's you can expect from me:

1) Discover a common marketing mistake that is keeping your business stuck.
2) Unlock a key strategy to help bust out of your stuck.
3) Access proven systems that will help streamline your advertising efforts and put you well on your way to nurturing the relationship you have with your buyers.

The Online Sales Mistake Most Businesses Make (and What to Do About It)

A few years ago I was asked by a local non-profit to help out with their call bank for a night of fundraising. I had never done cold calling before and I had no idea what I was in for.

The first thing that surprised me was how many calls I had to make before somebody answered the phone.

The second thing that I learned was that just about every person I talked to (even the really nice ones) were pretty annoyed that I had called and interrupted them from whatever it was that they were doing.....especially since I had interrupted them to ask for money.

I left that night with a definite respect for any person that has a cold calling requirement as part of the job.

Fast forward to the world of online marketing and sales, and everywhere you look you see the digital version of cold-calling... and it's just about as effective.

Tell me, how many ads have you seen while killing time on Facebook/Instagram/LinkedIn/name TheSocialNetwork, and after you click through, you're taken direct to a sales pitch... or worse, straight to an order page?

This is the online equivalent of going to a party and someone interrupting a conversation with your friend to tell you about a great deal they've got on timeshares.

You think, "ew", and bail to find the friend who just walked away.

<u>And people wonder why their conversion rates are so low.</u>

This is essentially what people are doing when they send cold traffic–i.e., strangers–straight to a sales page. Seriously, it's just as icky.
The good news is that the solution is easy to understand and implement, but before I get to that…

<u>…let's talk about why the direct ad-to-sales-page approach isn't very effective.</u>

The Problem with Hitting Someone Up Right Away

According to a Baylor University study[1] on the effectiveness of cold calling, they found it takes about fifty-nine answered cold calls to get a single qualified appointment or referral.

---

[1] Lampertz, Dale. "Has Cold Calling Gone Cold?," Baylor.edu, Keller Center Research Report , 01.01.2017 http://www.baylor.edu/content/services/document.php/183060 .pdf,

That's 118 answered cold calls for every two appointments.

Online marketing is similar to in-person marketing in a lot of ways–the main difference being the internet's fourth wall separating the prospect from the seller.

This fourth wall makes social customs even more important, because you can't depend on the salesperson's in-person charm and charisma to trigger social norms that would keep the prospect engaged.

What does that mean?

Well, if your ad shows up in a prospect's social media news feed, you're essentially interrupting a conversation. If your ad is interesting enough to get the prospect to click on it, *there'd better be something really outstanding on the other side to justify the interruption.*

Trust me when I say that "something outstanding" almost never means a sales or order page.

The typical online "cold call" is essentially an ad placement leading straight to a sales page (most common) or an order page (most brazen).

Sometimes this works, like when someone is in a buying frame of mind. This is why PPC ads and keywords can be so expensive–you're competing with everyone else to capture the hot buyers.

But most people just aren't there yet... you need to build trust.

But I'm getting ahead of myself.

Unless They're in the Right Mindset, a "Buy" Page is a Big Turnoff

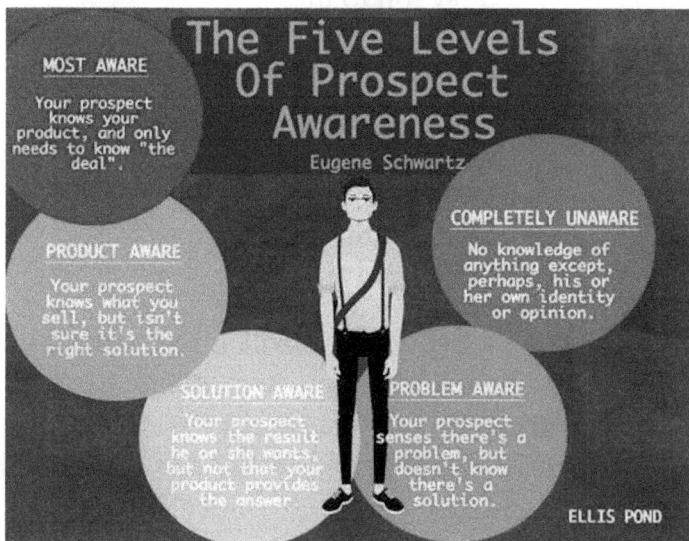

The infographic above illustrates legendary copywriter Eugene Schwartz's[2] theory that there are five levels of prospect awareness:

1. <u>Most Aware.</u> Your prospect knows your product, and only needs to know the "deal".
2. <u>Product Aware</u>. Your prospect knows what you sell, but isn't sure it's right for them.
3. <u>Solution Aware</u>. Your prospect knows the result he or she wants, but not that your product can deliver it to them.
4. <u>Problem Aware</u>. Your prospect senses she has a problem, but doesn't know there's a solution.
5. <u>Completely Unaware</u>. No knowledge of anything except– <u>maybe</u>–her own identify or opinion.

If you're sending traffic made up of people in the most aware category to a sales page or order page–and you're offering the solution to their burning problem–you're doing just fine.

---

[2] Schwartz, Eugene. *Breakthrough Advertising*, Bottom Line Books, 2004.

But the other four awareness levels need much more work than just presenting an offer…

They either don't trust you enough…

Don't know you exist…

Don't know there's a solution to their problem…

Or have no clue they even have a problem.
<u>If you send those last four groups of people to an order page, you're just wasting your money.</u>

The Biggest Reason Selling on the First Contact is a Losing Proposition (and the Quickest Way Around It)

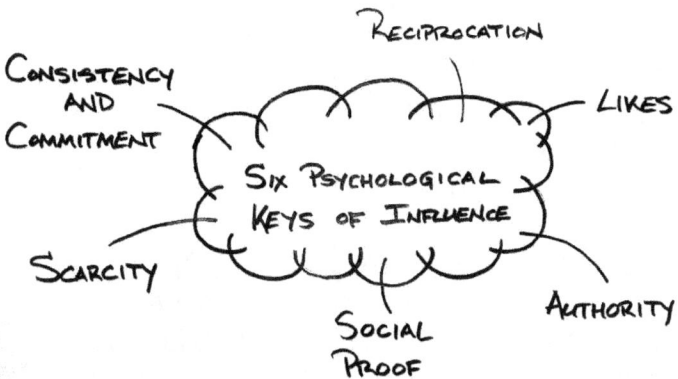

According to Robert Cialdini, famed expert on the psychology of persuasion, there are six influencers that tap into automatic processes in our brains, and are most likely to get you a favorable marketing outcome (i.e., your prospect buying your product).

1. Reciprocation
2. Commitment and consistency
3. Social proof
4. Liking
5. Authority
6. Scarcity

You want to use as many of these influencing principles as possible, but the quickest way to build rapport with people who don't know you is to give them something without asking for anything in return.

When someone gives us something without expecting anything back, we feel a sense of gratitude and debt towards the gift-giver. This "emotional debt" is called reciprocity, and is a powerful influencer when trying to warm up strangers to you and your brand.

Add that to the power of the "like" principle, and these prospects are likely to grow fond of you, increase their trust in you, and be more receptive when you finally present an offer to them.

But here's the kicker…

<u>The gift must be given without the expectation of anything in return.</u>

Violating this rule means the person will not feel that sense of emotional debt, and will think you're a manipulator.

How Do You Transform Cold Lurkers into Warm Prospects?

The key question is how to transform people who've never heard of you into happy additions to your list… and eventually customers.

There are four steps that are critical to attracting your ideal prospect (and repelling people you don't want to work with).

First, Let Them Decide

A whole lot is wrapped up into this first step: advertisement, image/video, copy, angle, message, offer, context, ad location, mindset of reader…

There's a whole lot going on here that we'll dig into deeper on a different day.

For now, let's just call it the ad.

If we're talking about cold traffic, the prospect is somebody who's never heard of you before.

This step is critical, because you want it to attract your best people—and annoy the people you don't want to work with.

With that in mind, the best thing you can do is be yourself—you'll attract like-minded people. Next, you want to get their attention.

Is your target audience stay-at-home moms who love knitting?
Call them out:

"Attention: Put Down That Knitting Needle! If You're a Stay-At-Home Mom Who Loves Knitting, This May Be the Most Important Message You See Today"

It doesn't have to be <u>that</u> dramatic, but you get my point.

Any man who reads the ad is probably going to ignore it.

Any woman who fits that description will at least look at it, and depending on the ad placement, the image, and the offer, they may click over to find out what the fuss is all about.

If the ad does its job, <u>people will self-identify themselves as interested prospects.</u>

Which is exactly what you want.

Second, Build Trust by Giving

This is where a lot of mistakes are made. Instead of trying to build a relationship with the prospect, many companies try to sell right away.

As we saw from the infographic earlier, there are times when that makes sense, like when your prospect knows what they want and they are ready and eager to buy.

But for the other folks who aren't ready to go whole hog, you need to build trust. And <u>there's no faster way of doing that then giving a valuable gift.</u>

If somebody takes you up on an offer for a free doodad–something that's so good they'd pay for it in different circumstances– they you've just taken advantage of a psychological principle that makes the person feel some sort of emotional debt toward you. (For more on the topic, I recommend Robert Cialdini's seminal work, Influence: The Psychology of Persuasion.)[3]

---

[3] Cialdini, Robert B. *Influence: The Psychology of Persuasion*, Harper Business; Revised edition, 2006.

As long as they feel that you're an honest dealer, this emotional debt is like a shortcut to trustworthiness.

Third, Stay Top of Mind

Depending on the **type of buyer**[4] you're dealing with, your prospect may take a long time to move from their position as a looker to that of a buyer.

No worries... just keep in touch with them.
If you send your audience good info on a regular basis, you'll build trust and be on the top of the list when they finally decide to buy what you're selling.

The easiest way to get this done is with an email autoresponder, and it doesn't take a ton of time—especially if you're emailing once or twice a week.

Fourth, Give Them a Reason to Buy

Don't kill your audience by selling to them all the time.

Remember, you're developing a relationship.

---

[4] Shultz, Mike. "The 6 Buyer Personas (and How to Sell to Them)," rainsalestraining.com, 01.02.201, http://www.rainsalestraining.com/blog/the-6-buyer-personas-and-how-to-sell-to-them

Think about your prospects as you'd think about a friend.

How fun is it to be around someone who's always asking for stuff? Well, it might not be that big of a deal if they're a good friend, need the help, etc. But what if you ask for help and they're never available? Well, now that friend is a moocher, and you're not going to go out of your way for that person in the future.

Business is the same.

If you keep hitting people up to buy your stuff, they're going to tune you out really fast.
However, if you are always giving... advice, tips, free downloads, etc., then your offers become that much more powerful when your audience sees them.

Of course, the offer has to be good—but if you've made regular deposits of value, you'll at least have their attention when you're selling.

I've Been Hinting at Simple Ways to Attract Clients Online...

By the way, each step I just described is just a marketing funnel step. (I'm so tricky...)

Let's put it all together!

Funnel Step 1: Let the Prospect Decide

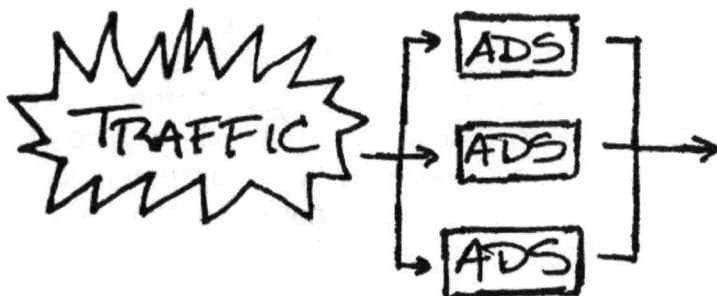

Funnel Step 2: Build Trust by Giving

Funnel Step 3: Stay Top of Mind

Funnel Step 4: Give A Compelling Reason to Buy

Now Put It All Together...

That's your funnel map!

Now we'll see one of these in the wild.

Let's See This in Action in the Real World…

This is a funnel sequence used by a reputable online marketing resource to capture people interested in learning how to identify their ideal prospects online. They offer a free avatar worksheet to help you get a solid picture of who your ads need to target, then make an offer on your way to getting your download that lets people self-identify as interested buyers or researchers/learners.

Let's walk through what they did…

The Ad: Letting People Decide

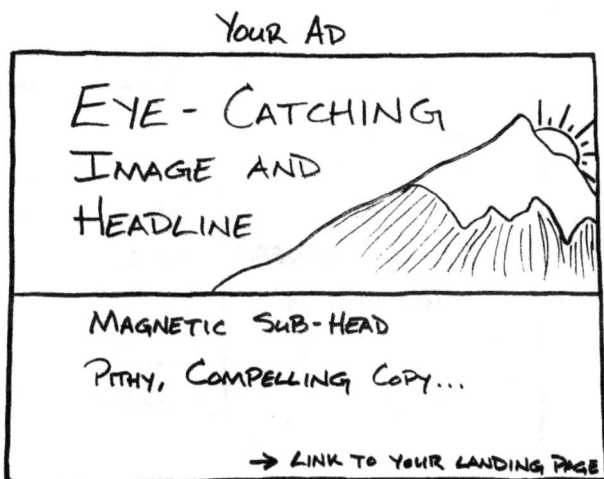

YOUR AD

EYE - CATCHING
IMAGE AND
HEADLINE

MAGNETIC SUB-HEAD

PITHY, COMPELLING COPY...

→ LINK TO YOUR LANDING PAGE

I saw this ad on the right side of my Facebook newsfeed. The ad appeals to anybody interested in running ads to generate leads, but who need a little help defining who they should target with their ads.

Once you click the ad, you're taken to step two, the landing page.

The Landing Page: Build Trust by Giving

What I love about this landing page is it doesn't assume that because you clicked on the ad, you're automatically going to trade your contact information for the free thingy they're pushing.

Instead, it's a full-on sales page that sells you on the benefits of the free download and builds up your interest in gaining the value the download offers you.

Which leads us to an upsell page in-between the opt-in (this page), and the download page...

The Upsell Page: Letting People Decide (again)

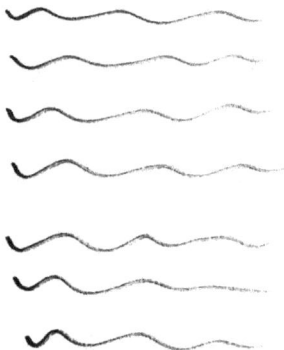

UPSELL PAGE

ALMOST THERE...

NEW PRODUCT

HEADLINE THAT EMPHASIZES THE BENEFITS CUSTOMERS RECEIVE

SUB-HEADLINE

SALES COPY

YES! I WANT THIS PRODUCT!

NO, I'M SATISFIED WITH MY CURRENT SITUATION

The genius of this page is that the new subscriber already feels like they got something for free, even though they haven't received it yet.

New subscribers see a low-cost offer that lets them choose how deep they want to go. Do they just want to use the free avatar download or do they want to take their business to a whole other level?

Each subscriber feels like they're getting an amazing deal (in this case the offer is 85% off the normal price); for the company running this funnel, they're getting a new paying customer they can market to over and over again.

This is key because once somebody buys, they're more likely to buy from you again.

Now after all this, you finally get your stuff.

Download Page: Build Trust by Giving

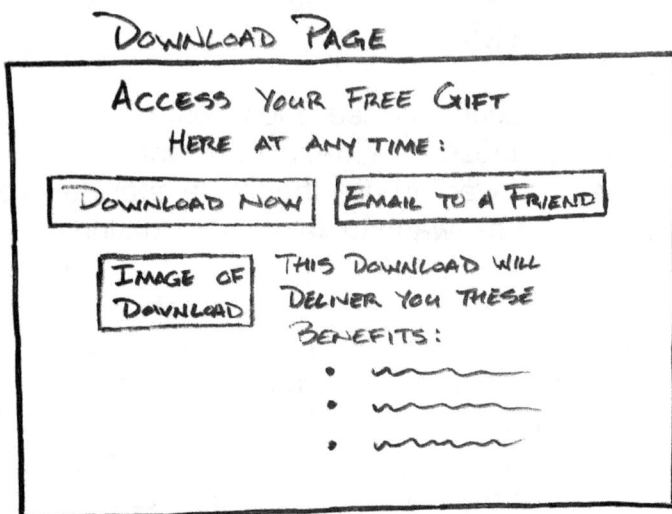

I love this download page: not only do you get your free thingy, but there's another bullet list reminding you why it's amazing (in case you forgot while admiring the upsell page.) This reinforces that you just received a valuable gift for free, and makes a deposit into each new subscriber's "trust account."

Stay Top Of Mind

The step you don't see is the email autoresponder sequence and the retargeting ads that ensure I don't forget that they gave me something valuable, that they have content I might be interested, and that they offer products that I might like to buy.

This step is crucial, and you can find more information about this step on my website ellispond.com.

Rearrange the Steps to Suit Your Needs

The is a great illustration showing you that the elements of the map I drew above is not set in stone; you can move the pieces as you see fit. Here's the breakdown of the funnel built by our reputable online marketing source.

Their list-building funnel flowed as follows:

1. Let people decide (ad)
2. Build trust by giving (opt-in)
3. Let people decide (upsell)
4. Build trust by giving (download page)
5. Stay top of mind (autoresponder… not seen)

You Can Follow This Model in Any Industry…

Just for kicks (and so you can see that this model works for industries outside of online marketing), I came up with some <u>client attraction ideas</u> so you can see that this model can work regardless of your business.

I wrote out some notes for seven different types of companies:

- Art gallery
- Chiropractor
- Dentist
- Logistics
- Optometrist
- Roofer
- Software developer

Since this chapter is already pretty long, I've made the notes about those seven company types available as a PDF download.

Go here if you'd like a copy: https://achieve.ellispond.com/client-attraction-notes

In the PDF, I give you my thoughts on how you can use this strategy in each of those businesses.

Even if your business is different from those seven, I think it's a wide enough range of business types that it will spark some ideas for you.

Wrapping Up

Developing relationships with your prospects rather than trying to have a transactional interaction with them just makes sense.
And with marketing automation software, building such a nurture funnel isn't as hard as it was even four years ago.

With the systems available to you that make automation easy, plus the benefits of adding a nurture strategy that warms up cold prospects, this is something you have to include in your lead generation roadmap.

- <u>More of the People Who Stick Around Will Become Customers.</u> Trust-building means you'll enjoy higher conversion rates, and longer-term engagements.
- <u>You'll Move Above the Fog of Your Commoditized Competitors.</u> Your customers will see you as a trusted resource–someone they refer their friends to–rather than merely a vendor or service provider. You're the trusted expert in your field.
- <u>Customers Will Stay with You Longer... and Buy More Often.</u> The lifetime value of each customer will skyrocket as clients stick around, reducing churn rates,

and as they buy more of your products and services.

The extra time and effort to put systems in place to develop and nurture these relationships is an investment well worth the price: http://www.ellispond.com/funnels/online-sales-mistake/ - respond

―――

Juliana Stachurski

Juliana Stachurski is the Owner and CEO of Ellis Pond Digital Marketing whose mission is to take marketing beyond aesthetics and utilize performance-driven techniques to optimize client messaging. She sets the strategy and vision to provide scalable strength for small to midsize business which allows those businesses to attract their best customers in ways that make selling a natural next step in the relationship. Her recent work includes driving eight figures in new revenue for the number one growing business in Tennessee and speaking at Bridgestone Arena for the UnStuck Nashville Conference. Originally from Seattle, WA., Juliana lives with her husband, eight children and a very large dog in Franklin, TN.

4

I'm Stuck With Not Enough Cash Flow Where Is My Cash? How Can We Get More?

Cash! It is the ultimate measuring stick for you and your business. The lack of cash is usually one of the primary reasons that businesses become stuck—or at least it is the one that finally gets your attention and causes you to reexamine your business differently.

Cash provides freedom for you and your business. Cash determines your ability to act within your business and on a personal basis. Cash is the grease/oil/lubrication that we all depend upon **AND** a continuing positive flow will create Excess Cash. Things become much simpler when there is Excess Cash in our bank accounts (including the business and personal)—your business operates as a well-oiled vehicle. You are able to drive it most anywhere and anytime. Excess Cash provides freedom and enables you to do more.

How can I transform my business into one of these well-oiled Cash Generating vehicles? I am certain that is everyone's goal and objective. You must have a plan and make it a priority – because there will be time periods/seasons, circumstances, and decisions that will consume your Cash. Before we dive into those weeds, there are some basic facts that we need to review. Afterwards, we will explore some proven methods that will help build a plan that will control and grow your Cash.

I am assuming that you own/control/manage a business enterprise. It does not matter whether your Company has over 100 employees or you are a Solopreneur—these basic principles remain the same. They apply to all For Profit and Non-Profit Companies. It does not matter whether you are structured as a LLC, C or S Corporation or Partnership/Proprietorship. They apply to Companies in: Real Estate and General Contractors; Banking, Insurance and Financial Firms; HealthCare Companies; Manufacturers and Fabricators; IT and all forms of Consulting Firms; whatever market your business serves. Whether it is sixty-one years old or a startup in a business incubator, these fundamental principles apply:

- Your Business is your greatest asset and cash generating vehicle;
- One of Its greatest benefit is the stream of Cash that it has generated, currently generating and will continue to generate;
- The sustainability and certainty and your Cash Flow determines the value of your business;
- The established companies with stable and less risky Cash Flow will realize a value premium compared to those that have more risk and uncertainty;
- Now let's focus on Cash and then building a Plan that will expand your Cash Flow!

What is Cash? Cash refers to the money in the physical form of currency—I will not go down the rabbit hole describing how currency is rapidly evolving. We need to focus on the movement of Cash—our flow of Cash. Investopedia defines Cash Flow as the amount of cash and cash equivalents moving into and out of a business' bank account. We know that a steady and dependable stream of **Positive** Cash Flow makes everything in your life work better. It is so simple: **Positive** Cash Flow is generated when your incoming Cash exceeds your outgoing cash. But simple is not reality—customers pay late, suppliers want early payment plus the payroll, and overhead costs keep increasing. Operations tells you that a critical piece of equipment is down and it needs to be repaired or replaced—capital and other needs keep popping to gobble your cash! Before we can make sense of all these conflicting factors we need to review how your business generates the financial information that is used. This helps us understand the process and their drivers. It is the first step towards seizing control of your Cash Flow!

Who prepares your financial information? What is their background and experience? We need to learn about their primary focus. During my thirty-eight-year financial career, I found that a majority of the bookkeepers/ accountants/ tax preparers/ controllers typically deal with yesterday and today. Their focus is classifying the financial transactions and events from yesterday, last week, last month, last year, etc. They are primarily historians; their role demands them to be accurate with a great attention to detail. These financial experts are **Reactive** and are most comfortable dealing with known information. They prepare the standard GAAP (Generally Accepted Accounting Principles) accrual based financial statements: Income Statement and Balance Sheet. Their information is critically important and vital to the success of your business—everyone needs this data and these reports. However, a different mindset and focus is necessary to change the future of your business and improve its Cash Flow. A **Proactive** mindset is required to transform your business' Cash Flow. You need a proactive financial professional that will roll their sleeves up, apply a holistic approach to understanding your business, and help you build a financial model that will map your companies' expected financial futures. This Plan is the first step towards gaining control of your Cash Flow and improving the profitability and financial fortune of your company.

In order to have a successful plan, you need answers to the following three questions:

1. Where Are You?
2. Where Are Going?
3. How Are We Going to Do It?

These simple questions are vital to getting your business UnStuck. Let's unpack each one of them to ask some penetrating questions. Your improved Cash Flow will depend on it.

Where Are You? Your financial history has a wealth of information in it. You can develop trends for most items in your financials (I like to use the last thirty-six months). There are several elements that need some special attention:

1. **<u>Sales:</u>** Dollar Amount, By Customer, By Product Line; Average Pricing by Product—the sales by customer and product will help you quickly determine Who is buying and What they are buying. The 80/20 Rule will identify and affirm your more important customers and products.

2. **<u>Accounts Receivables:</u>** Dollar Amount; Customer Name; Invoice Age; Payment Terms—the Days Sales Outstanding (DSO) can quickly be computed with this information. The DSO will identify the Customers that take too long to pay their bills? Examine your A/R history so you can determine whether there was special circumstance or they are problem payers. Be firm and diligent with the ones that are taking too long (refer to their profitability in #3).

3. **<u>Gross Profit:</u>** Dollar Amount; By Customer; By Product Line/Project; Average Pricing by Product/Project – **this is the most important line item for any business**.

Each business is unique, but they all use the following components:

    a. **Materials:** What are the Average Cost for raw materials for your products (refer to the more important ones from #1)? Do you have a long lead time obtaining these goods? How do you track them through Inventory?

    b. **Direct Labor:** How much Labor is required? How many employees are required for each unity? What do they cost you by hour? Is there a surplus or shortage of talented employees?

    c. **Other Direct Costs:** Each business may have other miscellaneous costs (supplies, freight, equipment rental, etc.). What are the average costs that are incurred?

It is critical to learn the Average Gross Profit by Customer and by Product. This will help you determine Profitability of your Customers and Product Line. This data will help you make better decisions with facts. I have witnessed many companies significantly improve their profits and Cash Flow by eliminating an unprofitable Customer or Product Line.

4. **Accounts Payable:** Dollar Amount, Vendor Name, Invoice Age; Payment Terms—the Age of the Invoice can quickly be computed

with this information. Segment your Vendors by their importance to your product/service. Keep the vital ones paid. It will help you negotiate on price reductions or better terms later. Determine which Vendors will accept credit card payments. Pay them with credit cards – you can receive benefits/points and get an additional period of float. PLEASE pay your credit card – this is expensive financing!

5. **Inventory:** Dollar Amount by Inventory Item; Number of Units; Average Age – significant amounts of cash get stuck in Inventory. Work on streamlining your process to minimize the amount of inventory required. Increasing the Inventory turns will generate Cash for your company.

6. **EBITDA:** This means Earnings Before Interest Taxes, Depreciation and Amortization and also called Net Operating Income. It approximates the Cash Flow Profit generated by your business. We want this amount to be as high as possible. Bankers use EBITDA to determine the level of bank debt that your business can afford.

7. **Overhead Expenses:** The Total Overhead Expenses required to operate your business. Here is a listing of the most common expenses incurred:

   a. **Total Payroll:** Verify that all non-Direct Labor employees and prospective new hires are included with their expected Average Salary Increases. It has been my experience to keep all these costs in a single area—plus include all Management/Owners Compensation in the total.

b. **Payroll Taxes & Related Employee Expenses:** Employer Payroll Taxes plus any additional costs provided by the Company (health insurance, retirement matching, education reimbursements, worker's compensation, etc.). I suggest that you plan for significant increases in employee medical insurance premiums.

c. **Sales & Marketing:** Additional costs required to sell and promote your products/services.

d. **Rent & Occupancy:** Total Rent, Utilities, Telephone, Internet and related costs associated with all your office locations.

e. **Professional Fees:** Total Professional Fees costs for legal, consulting, accounting & tax preparation services.

f. **Business Insurance:** Total cost for Business Liability Insurance and Other Forms of Insurance.

g. **General Administrative & Office:** Total cost for Office Expenses &

Supplies, Printing & Stationary, Postage & Overnight, Bank Charges & Fees, IT & Software Costs, Travel, Auto Maintenance and Miscellaneous Costs.

Now you have a solid foundation for transforming your business. All areas are being tracked and measured. We will be able to see the impact of our future changes.

Where Are You Going? You have a sense where your business is headed. Ask your Management Team and valued employees their expectations. Their intuitive sense will help you – understand that it may be limited to their piece of your business.

How Are We Going to Do It? Now you know the decisions that need to be made. Can you hit your goal staying on your current course? What changes will be necessary and required? You need to build at least three years of monthly proformas that capture your vision. This is a customized financial plan that maps out the path/road your business must travel to attain your goals. I suggest that it mirror your three years of financial history that you developed in **Where Are We**. There are some fundamentals that are required to improve your Cash Flow and Profitability:

1. **Improve Gross Profit as a Percent of Sales** – this will be realized through more efficient operations; gradual and strategic price increases and elimination of problem/unprofitable customers;
2. **Establish Increased Levels of EBITDA** – greater profits have to be expected, planned and nurtured. Review the historical performances of EBITDA as a % Sales and set significant targets;
3. **Reduction of Overhead Expenses** – consistently verify the need for each additional dollar of overhead. A dollar of overhead saved is a dollar of profit/cash!
4. **Monitor Working Capital** – reduce Accounts Receivable/Inventory and use (don't abuse) your vendors and credit cards.

I suggest that you examine your Better/(Worse) Variance Analysis (Comparison of Actual vs. Plan performance on a Monthly and Year–to-Date basis). This definitively shows your progress towards your goal. These reports are your financial guardrails. They let us know when an assumption is invalid. We use this information to research, develop corrective and immediate action. This help you break through the obstacles that will challenge your business and its goals.

This path and approach will improve your Cash Flow and financial performance. However, there are circumstances when that is not enough and I reach out to my friend, Terry Luker. Terry can help you get your business recapitalized. I know, I saw, I witnessed, and my client benefited. Let's learn how Terry can get you a bigger Cash Flow pipe!

Have you figured out the biggest need your new business is going to have? It's not your creative juices running wild, although that would be a great help. It's not making sure that you hire world class people, although that would also be a great help. It's not even delivering a world class product that you perfect better than anyone else, although that too would be a great help.

Simply put, the biggest need your business will have is cash flow. Notice I did not say profitability, although profitability is something all lenders want to see from you as quickly as possible. The biggest need you will have as a small business owner is going to be your cash flow. Cash flow will allow you to stay in business, pay those world-class people you are hiring, keep your world-class product flowing, and most important, cash flow allows you to stay focused on your business and keep those creative juices flowing.

The number one reason businesses fail is that they run out of money. Now, I understand that many people will say businesses fail for other reasons such as poor leadership, a poor product or design, or even a poorly executed plan. Those can be some of the reasons, but the bottom line is that when a company runs out of money, it must close. All those other reasons may be mitigating factors in leading up to running out of money, but the number ONE reason businesses close is that they run out of money.

Even before the company runs out of money, the business owner is spending all their time chasing capital (money) to keep the business open and operating is a complete drain on the entrepreneurial spirit of the company. When you are focused on raising capital (cash flow), you are not focused on the operations of your company. You can't look ahead and see the ebb and flow of the business community that affects the future growth and well-being of your company. You don't see changes in trends with consumers and you are no longer out there on the cutting edge making sure your company stays current and relevant. You simply get tired of the day-to-day grind of looking for money to keep your company up and running. Instead of thinking and planning for the glorious future you envisioned when you opened your company, you start to think about scaling back, laying people off, and shrinking down your new company.

All of this takes the focus off your business and, thus, your business begins to slide. Employees and vendors begin to see a difference in you. Without yet running out of money, your business is on a steep decline because it lost its number one cheerleader and visionary—you—to being a money chaser.

The sad part of this is most business owners never realize it's just as important to have a plan in place to provide funding for your company as it is to have a plan in place to provide your product to the public. There are several stages of funding that every business is going to go through. Knowing those stages and understanding the need to have those stages and plans in place is critical to the success of every business owner in America. If you plan poorly, your business is going to perform poorly. If you plan strategically for this part of your business plan, the business has an opportunity to soar and will certainly not be held back due to the lack of capital.

Most new businesses today get started using a combination of funding through one of the following sources: (a) Through the business owner's own savings; (b) through family and friends; and/or (c) through a loan from a lending institution.

I think we can agree that (a) and (b) are self-explanatory. I want to discuss the loan through a lending institution. In discussing lending institutions, I want to focus on banks as they are the cheapest way to obtain financing for your business. There are other avenues such as hedge funds, hard money lenders, and venture capitalists, but those routes are very expensive and normally require high interest rate loans with not very appealing terms to new business owners. Those sources can also require the business owners to give up operational control of the business and therefore take away the business owners entrepreneurial spirit.

Obtaining a loan from a bank is certainly not a given for any business owner. Many people believe it's easier to get a loan once you have been in business for a while when, in fact, due to the Small Business Administration (SBA), it can often be easier to get a loan as a startup business than as an ongoing business. Here is the reason why. When you are a startup business, you get the opportunity to prepare a pro forma on your business—a business plan with projections on how your business is going to be run and how your business is going to perform. Many times, this is simply an educated (as much as possible) guess.

Once you have opened your business and are up and running, you can no longer get loans based on the pro forma of your business (the educated guess plan); you must use your current profit and loss statements and the actual performance of your business. The lender is going to want to see how you started, how you're doing and only then will they take under consideration where you might be going. The issue here is that most businesses in the first two to three years are not going to be profitable. Unfortunately, that is when businesses need the access to capital the most. Getting through those "cash burn" periods of your new business—that is you have more cash going out than you have coming in—is one of the most critical phases of your business.

On many occasions, companies approach us to help them with their cash flow (they need a loan) only to discover they have been placed in a very poorly structured SBA loan. Once a business is in an SBA loan, it is very hard to get that company the cash they need to grow and expand. SBA loans normally tie up all assets of the business owner as well as future cash flows and assets with a blanket lien on all those assets. Please understand that I am not bashing SBA loans. They are a life-line for small business owners. What I am saying is that most banks claim they do SBA loans and understand SBA loans when, in fact, most do not. Many banks go so far as to "farm out" their entire SBA loan process to third parties. The main issue with SBA funding is that many banks do not allow for enough working capital to ensure the business will get to the point of having positive cash flow and then be self-supporting. Too many banks and lenders want to scale back available funds to the business owner instead of having the knowledge to look at the client's business plan, understand it, and make sure there is enough working capital to sustain the company through the "cash burn."

So, where do you go? Well, there are two different paths. If you are a business owner who is just starting out, a well-funded SBA loan can be the beginning of a great business that changes your life and your families' lives for generations to come. However, I would use the SBA process as a last resort for funding my business. A traditional bank loan using some of your existing assets and cash flows would be my preference for beginning your business.

If you are an existing business and in need of additional cash to grow and expand your business (aren't we all), I would recommend finding a partner who understands lending and is not going to charge you upfront fees to get the cash you need to grow your business. The cash you need to grow your business can come in several forms, but here are the two we work with the most:

1. Many times, business owners have the assets they need to grow and expand their business and their cash flows. Often what we encounter is that the business owner's assets are misaligned with his or her business needs. For example, one client had an abundance of equity in his real estate holdings but needed that equity in his operating account so that he could expand his sales. We were simply able to reconstruct his existing debt in such a way as to provide additional cash into his operating account while at the same time we negotiated better terms on the old debt that increased his cash flows and reduced his overall monthly payment on the debt even after adding the new debt to the equation. Remember, cash flow is affected by an increase or a reduction in debt just as it is by an increase in sales (if you can maintain your expenses).

   Having the debt structure of a company "right sized" so that the company can grow and prosper can be just as important to cash flow as it is to go out and secure additional lines of credit for operational needs. The idea about cash flow is to grow your pipeline of cash to the levels you need to allow your business to grow.

2. Often business owners have other collateral that we can use to obtain additional lines of credit, working capital loans and other alternative funding options to assist in the growth of that company. You must remember that each situation requires its own evaluation from someone who is not emotionally tied to the recommendations that are presented to the business owner. I can remember meeting with one business owner that after we had completed our visit, the decision was that the owner just wanted to sell the business and retire. There is no sense in taking on more debt if you do not have a plan to put that debt to great use and grow and expand the company. As important as securing additional cash flow for your company may be, you must have a plan to use that additional cash flow and to make sure that you have the discipline to payoff that debt as soon as you can. The most profitable businesses in the world are the ones with the least amount of debt.

Debt is something that almost every business owner is going to have to deal with unless you have rich family members with deep pockets. Cash flow is something that every business owner must be aware of and must learn to manage. Debt and cash flow are items that you might normally think do not go together, but a great business owner understands that both must be managed. Sometime we must take on additional debt to save, grow and or expand our businesses. Those decisions should not be made lightly. In our business world, most banks only want to lend to companies that do not need the money. If you are looking to increase your cash flow through additional debt, you need to have a great plan of how that debt will increase your sales and ultimately your profitability to convince the lender to give you the loan. If this is the track you are taking, then you will need the help of a business visionary like Steve Byington to help put the numbers and plan together so that the plan can be "sold" to a lender.

Cash flow is the life blood of any business and the ONLY reason businesses fail is that they run out of cash. There are many ways to increase your cash flow. A business commercial loan specialist working with a great business cash analyst is a great place to start.

5

The Number One Reason Businesses Fail Is That They Run Out of Money

Have you figured out the biggest need your new business is going to have? It's not your creative juices running wild, although that would be a great help. It's not making sure that you hire world class people, although that would also be a great help. It's not even delivering a world class product that you perfect better than anyone else, although that too would be a great help.

Simply put, the biggest need your business will have is cash flow. Notice I did not say profitability, although profitability is something all lenders want to see from you as quickly as possible. The biggest need you will have as a small business owner is going to be your cash flow. Cash flow will allow you to stay in business, pay those world-class people you are hiring, keep your world-class product flowing, and most important, cash flow allows you to stay focused on your business and keep those creative juices flowing.

The number one reason businesses fail is that they run out of money. Now, I understand that many people will say businesses fail for other reasons such as poor leadership, a poor product or design, or even a poorly executed plan. Those can be some of the reasons, but the bottom line is that when a company runs out of money, it must close. All those other reasons may be mitigating factors in leading up to running out of money, but the number ONE reason businesses close is that they run out of money.

Even before the company runs out of money, the business owner is spending all their time chasing capital (money) to keep the business open and operating is a complete drain on the entrepreneurial spirit of the company. When you are focused on raising capital (cash flow), you are not focused on the operations of your company. You can't look ahead and see the ebb and flow of the business community that affects the future growth and well-being of your company. You don't see changes in trends with consumers and you are no longer out there on the cutting edge making sure your company stays current and relevant. You simply get tired of the day-to-day grind of looking for money to keep your company up and running. Instead of thinking and planning for the glorious future you envisioned when you opened your company, you start to think about scaling back, laying people off, and shrinking down your new company.

All of this takes the focus off your business and, thus, your business begins to slide. Employees and vendors begin to see a difference in you. Without yet running out of money, your business is on a steep decline because it lost its number one cheerleader and visionary—you—to being a money chaser.

The sad part of this is most business owners never realize it's just as important to have a plan in place to provide funding for your company as it is to have a plan in place to provide your product to the public. There are several stages of funding that every business is going to go through. Knowing those stages and understanding the need to have those stages and plans in place is critical to the success of every business owner in America. If you plan poorly, your business is going to perform poorly. If you plan strategically for this part of your business plan, the business has an opportunity to soar and will certainly not be held back due to the lack of capital.

Most new businesses today get started using a combination of funding through one of the following sources: (a) Through the business owner's own savings; (b) through family and friends; and/or (c) through a loan from a lending institution.

I think we can agree that (a) and (b) are self-explanatory. I want to discuss the loan through a lending institution. In discussing lending institutions, I want to focus on banks as they are the cheapest way to obtain financing for your business. There are other avenues such as hedge funds, hard money lenders, and venture capitalists, but those routes are very expensive and normally require high interest rate loans with not very appealing terms to new business owners. Those sources can also require the business owners to give up operational control of the business and therefore take away the business owners entrepreneurial spirit.

Obtaining a loan from a bank is certainly not a given for any business owner. Many people believe it's easier to get a loan once you have been in business for a while when, in fact, due to the Small Business Administration (SBA), it can often be easier to get a loan as a startup business than as an ongoing business. Here is the reason why. When you are a startup business, you get the opportunity to prepare a pro forma on your business—a business plan with projections on how your business is going to be run and how your business is going to perform. Many times, this is simply an educated (as much as possible) guess.

Once you have opened your business and are up and running, you can no longer get loans based on the pro forma of your business (the educated guess plan); you must use your current profit and loss statements and the actual performance of your business. The lender is going to want to see how you started, how you're doing and only then will they take under consideration where you might be going. The issue here is that most businesses in the first two to three years are not going to be profitable. Unfortunately, that is when businesses need the access to capital the most. Getting through those "cash burn" periods of your new business—that is you have more cash going out than you have coming in—is one of the most critical phases of your business.

On many occasions, companies approach us to help them with their cash flow (they need a loan) only to discover they have been placed in a very poorly structured SBA loan. Once a business is in an SBA loan, it is very hard to get that company the cash they need to grow and expand. SBA loans normally tie up all assets of the business owner as well as future cash flows and assets with a blanket lien on all those assets. Please understand that I am not bashing SBA loans. They are a life-line for small business owners. What I am saying is that most banks claim they do SBA loans and understand SBA loans when, in fact, most do not. Many banks go so far as to "farm out" their entire SBA loan process to third parties. The main issue with SBA funding is that many banks do not allow for enough working capital to ensure the business will get to the point of having positive cash flow and then be self-supporting. Too many banks and lenders want to scale back available funds to the business owner instead of having the knowledge to look at the client's business plan, understand it, and make sure there is enough working capital to sustain the company through the "cash burn."

So, where do you go? Well, there are two different paths. If you are a business owner who is just starting out, a well-funded SBA loan can be the beginning of a great business that changes your life and your families' lives for generations to come. However, I would use the SBA process as a last resort for funding my business. A traditional bank loan using some of your existing assets and cash flows would be my preference for beginning your business.

If you are an existing business and in need of additional cash to grow and expand your business (aren't we all), I would recommend finding a partner who understands lending and is not going to charge you upfront fees to get the cash you need to grow your business. The cash you need to grow your business can come in several forms, but here are the two we work with the most:

1. Many times, business owners have the assets they need to grow and expand their business and their cash flows. Often what we encounter is that the business owner's assets are misaligned with his or her business needs. For example, one client had an abundance of equity in his real estate holdings but needed that equity in his operating account so that he could expand his sales. We were simply able to reconstruct his existing debt in such a way as to provide additional cash into his

operating account while at the same time we negotiated better terms on the old debt that increased his cash flows and reduced his overall monthly payment on the debt even after adding the new debt to the equation. Remember, cash flow is affected by an increase or a reduction in debt just as it is by an increase in sales (if you can maintain your expenses).

Having the debt structure of a company "right sized" so that the company can grow and prosper can be just as important to cash flow as it is to go out and secure additional lines of credit for operational needs. The idea about cash flow is to grow your pipeline of cash to the levels you need to allow your business to grow.

2. Often business owners have other collateral that we can use to obtain additional lines of credit, working capital loans and other alternative funding options to assist in the growth of that company. You must remember that each situation requires its own evaluation from someone who is not emotionally tied to the recommendations that are presented to the business owner. I can remember meeting with one business owner that after we had completed our visit,

the decision was that the owner just wanted to sell the business and retire. There is no sense in taking on more debt if you do not have a plan to put that debt to great use and grow and expand the company. As important as securing additional cash flow for your company may be, you must have a plan to use that additional cash flow and to make sure that you have the discipline to payoff that debt as soon as you can. The most profitable businesses in the world are the ones with the least amount of debt.

Debt is something that almost every business owner is going to have to deal with unless you have rich family members with deep pockets. Cash flow is something that every business owner must be aware of and must learn to manage. Debt and cash flow are items that you might normally think do not go together, but a great business owner understands that both must be managed. Sometime we must take on additional debt to save, grow and or expand our businesses. Those decisions should not be made lightly. In our business world, most banks only want to lend to companies that do not need the money. If you are looking to increase your cash flow through additional debt, you need to have a great plan of how that debt will increase your sales and ultimately your profitability to convince the lender to give you the loan. If this is the track you are taking, then you will need the help of a business visionary like Steve Byington to help put the numbers and plan together so that the plan can be "sold" to a lender.

Cash flow is the life blood of any business and the ONLY reason businesses fail is that they run out of cash. There are many ways to increase your cash flow. A business commercial loan specialist working with a great business cash analyst is a great place to start.

6

Join Me on My Road to Becoming
a Super Hero

Do you ever catch yourself waking up in the
morning and the first thing you do, before
anything else, is reach for your phone and sift
through countless emails, deciding which is
pertinent and which can be discarded? I'm not
really sure when this habit began for me, but it
never fails—I wake up, check my phone, and
I'm immediately back in work mode. The pile of
things that need to be accomplished seem to
be ever-growing and never-ending. Time

needs to be spent on LinkedIn, research needs to be done, reports need to be prepared, and meetings need to be confirmed. Data seems to be streaming toward us from every direction. There doesn't seem to be enough time in the day to stay on top of everything that needs to be done. As a professional, I can never let my work performance suffer; as a husband and father, I cannot let the requirements take away from my family. So, who lost? I did. I stopped growing, stopped improving, and stopped looking for the next step to take.

Technology can either help us or hurt us in our effort to overcome the never-ending tug-of-war between work, family, and personal development. During the fifteenth and sixteenth centuries, a "New Birth" sprang up from the Dark Ages. During the Renaissance, there was a renewed interest in education and art. This movement helped society stop thinking as medieval men of the Dark Ages and begin thinking as modern men. Today, we are experiencing a new Dark Age where technology and work consume our lives. We have our smart phones and other technologies that help us accomplish more, but they also take so much more away from our lives and families. It is time for another "New Birth." It is time to take back our lives. It is time for us to become like A Super Hero by using technology to recover misplaced productivity and use it to develop our skills and increase our knowledge.

What is a Super Hero? Most of us have either grown up reading the comic books or have seen the recent super hero movies. He is a very intelligent, albeit sometimes arrogant, person who often technology and a virtual assistant to accomplish great things. Yes, he is a fictional character, but we have much of the same technology at our fingertips. We call it the smartphone.

Becoming A Super Hero begins with using the same technologies that monopolize our time and utilize them to enhance our lives. There are so many everyday tech tools that help us save the day. Smart phone apps help with expense and navigation, Office 365 apps allow us to work anywhere, and rules and workflows make things happen so we can focus on important items. Software shouldn't be something you spend a lot of time on or even think about. It should work in the background and optimize our time each day.

Let's look at seven everyday tech tools that improve productivity:

1. Email and Calendar Management
2. If This Then That
3. LinkedIn

4. Navigation
5. Expenses and Time Tracking
6. Microsoft Office App for Smart Devices
7. Shopping

Email and Calendar Management

Emails and calendars can overwhelm us and waste much of our day. Trying to find that lost email or making sure we respond to that very important contact can be time-consuming. There are several tools available to manage both and redeem hours in our day:

- Both Microsoft and Gmail have email rules that take only a few minutes to set up. After configuration, they will manage routine emails to keep the important ones in your inbox. Rules use basic logic; "if this happens, then do this."

- Microsoft has a relatively new tool called Clutter. It learns from your normal actions of read or ignore, then applies it to new ones. It will move the emails that you are most likely to ignore to the Clutter folder.

- Boomerang is a free app that integrates with either Microsoft or Gmail. With this tool, you can write an email, send it now, or schedule it to be sent at a future date and time. If there is no response to the email, then it is "boomeranged" back to the top of your email according to a pre-selected time period (i.e., 4 hours, 1 Day, 2 Days, etc.) This helps you stay on top of your emails, resulting in a cleaner inbox. Perhaps the best part of this tool is its scheduling function. It looks at your calendar, shows you when you're available, and allows you to send the recipient an invite showing your calendar. They select the time/date and both of you receive the invite.

- Another great scheduling tool is "New meeting tool." You make recommendations based on your calendar and send a link to the group you need to meet. They'll receive the email with the embedded link. They select from your recommendations or make their own recommendations. Once the group votes, you can select the best time for the majority of the group.

- One more tool, also by Microsoft, is the Office 365 (CRM). It is embedded into your email and calendar, allowing you to work within those tools and tracking needed data without having to enter the same data into another system.

If This Then That
Part of becoming A SUPER HERO is that the "routine" should just happen. Everyday tasks

can often be handled by technology; i.e., reports can be automated, work flows can be set or even electronics can be turned on or off. There are so many different tech tools that can handle the "routine," allowing you to focus on your important task. Here are two recommendations for just that. They are IFTTT (if this then that) and Microsoft Flow. Both of them interact with other apps and platforms again using the basic logic of "if this happens then do that." It is a very simple and elegant solution to many of our everyday tasks.

In IFTTT, the process is called a recipe. They can be made on the free smart phone app or the ifttt.com site. Here are a few examples:

If it is 5:30 a.m., then I receive a text with today's weather.

If I post a picture on Facebook with #SEBF, then the picture is also saved in a folder.

My favorite recipe was created by my son, Nathan. He always forgot to text us when he had made it back to the university. He created a recipe so that when he arrived to the longitude and latitude of his apartment, his Mom would receive a text that said "Made it back. Love you."

Microsoft Flow works similarly, but the recipes are called templates. It is free, but some functions work better with an Office 365 subscription. The main goal of Flow is to allow online collaboration with business people.

Both tools allow you to focus on the important items of your day while the routine tasks happen in the background. The recovery of a minute here, thirty seconds there adds up to a lot of wasted time you can apply to more important activities.

LinkedIn

LinkedIn is the largest professional online network in the world. With 467,000,000 members worldwide, it is a powerful tool for connecting with prospects and colleagues. The basic service of LinkedIn.com is free along with the app. I distinctly remember one day when I had a coffee meeting with a gentleman who was not up-to-date on technology. He still had a flip phone and was not on LinkedIn. I had another meeting scheduled at the same time, so luckily I was already there. Nearing the meeting time for the meeting, I received a text from my new prospect. "What are you wearing? I'm wearing khakis with a blue shirt." Gone are the days of that uncomfortable email or text request of "What are you wearing?" Simply access the LinkedIn app and look at the prospect's profile picture. **Note**: Don't be THAT guy without a current profile picture. The app is a great way to prep for a meeting by looking at the background and connections of your prospect. There are other daily actions you can utilize with LinkedIn that can save you a great deal of research time:

Notifications – each day I review the notifications from the app to find out and congratulate my contacts on business anniversaries, new positions, new jobs and birthdays. On a side note, I once thought that it was dumb and unprofessional to send birthday wishes through LinkedIn. I was wrong. Since I started wishing my professional network "Happy Birthday," I have reconnected with several contacts that I have not spoken with in a very long time.

LinkedIn Groups – by being a part of a LinkedIn Group, you can reach people outside of your professional network. Find a group that makes sense for you to be a member, then post relevant information. This is not a place to sell, but to share. Not long ago a company reached out to me because they needed a local partner. That company found me because of information that I had posted on a Group in LinkedIn.

LinkedIn Advanced Search – Create an advanced search identifying your point of contact, area of interest and keywords. Look for second connections only. You already know your first connections. After creating the search then save it and set it up to email you each week with any updates. As you and your network expand their professional network in LinkedIn, the search has new information. If the search generates people that interest you, then reach out to your first contact for an introduction.

Allowing LinkedIn to keep up and research your connections and prospects is another way to help technology get back part of your day.

Navigation

Do you remember entering addresses into your GPS, printing off maps, or better yet having an actual map in your car? Have you stood in the heat or rain waiting to pay for parking or paid way too much for a taxi? How about spent time looking up a new restaurant/coffee shop to have that next business meeting? Here are a few tools that may help:

There are several apps for the smart phone that work for your navigation, but I believe the

Waze is the leader of the pack. Waze picks up addresses from your calendar, gives you the best route to your meetings, and allows you to send ETA's to your team.

Uber and Lyft both have great apps for the smart phone that automatically call for a ride that is less expensive than a taxi. The app gives you an update of your ride, the tag number and name of the driver. The app is tied to your PayPal account, so no money is exchanged with the driver.

ParkMobile is an app to pay for parking. No more standing in line in the heat, rain or at night. Simply scan the QR code at the lot and it's done.

There are two very good apps that help with picking out that next coffee shop or restaurant - Yelp and TripAdvisor. Both are very easy to search and do a great job.

Once you start regaining your time, then we can begin expanding your knowledge and skills.

Enhancing your skills can increase your work productivity and position at work. **Becoming A Super Hero means becoming the best at**

what we do for a living and moving up the food chain. One of my ways I have coached people is by letting them know that "Life is a river, and there is a current. If you're treading water, then you are backing up."

Expenses & Time Tracking

All of us have business expenses, but tracking them can be so very time consuming. There are a few smart phone apps that can make tracking them just happen in the background. My main rule when dealing with my expenses is that the app has a website companion. I like having the control of the website to go along with the convenience of the phone app.

My primary app/website is Expensify. It tracks three things: receipts, mileage and time. Just take a picture of the receipt and attach it to the event. The result is a monthly report that can be exported to Excel that has pictures attached to document the expense. The mileage can be tracked or added later on the website, along with the time spent during a project. The system allows for an invoice to be produced to give to a client.

Expensify does a good job tracking mileage, but it is a little quirky. Perhaps a better app is MileIQ. It tracks everything in the background, and all you have to do is slide right in the screen if it is business trip or left for a personal one. The app provides a report for the month, plus an annual report for taxes. A bonus is that each month, you receive an emailed report of the business miles driven and the tax benefit.

For people that are self-employed, QuickBooks has an app that does the expense tracking along with the time. The bonus here is that the app is connected to your accounting system, enabling you to track expenses and invoice clients at the same time.

Microsoft Office on Your Smart Device

Microsoft apps takes being mobile and working from anywhere to the next level. If you go to your app store and search for Microsoft, you'll find a host of apps that can take you on the road. Here are a few:

Office Lens has become one of my favorite apps. It's a free app that allows you to take a photo of a document with your phone, then share it via email, save as a pdf or store in OneNote. You can take a photo of a whiteboard and share it the same way. The great thing about it is that it repositions and cleans up the edges. Lastly, the app can be used to scan business cards. After scanning the card, save it to OneNote, then to your contacts.

Skype for Business is similar to GoToMeeting, but now with integration into Office 365. Any meeting within your calendar can be converted into a conference call meeting with the link and numbers as well as all the video, screen settings and recording capabilities. Instant polling and quick surveys are a great tool as well. Additionally, Skype is the largest phone service in the world. One of the tools that makes life very easy when working with team member is knowing who's working in Outlook and being able to IM them without having to take the time for a call. No more having to worry if your team is working, you can check if they are active in Skype.

There are several CRM's on the market with some being very good and some not so much. The Microsoft Dynamic CRM has a very big advantage in that it is built by the same people that brought you your calendar and email. This CRM exists inside your calendar/email and you never have to leave it. This prevents users from having to track information in their CRM and repeat the same activity in their calendar/email. The ease of getting to the data has a direct relationship to improved customer service. I think we all have had the frustration of repeating the same information to our vendor every time you speak with them. Converting leads to opportunities and ultimately to sales becomes clearer and more fluid. When sales teams have to enter data into multiple sites, they tend to not keep track of everything. The real information is in their calendar and not the CRM. When the systems are one and the same, it helps the sales teams stay on track and allows management to have the information they need. Because the CRM is in your calendar, adding contacts and leads to marketing lists is easy, and so is tracking all your marketing activity for each. I think the best advantage for the Microsoft Dynamic CRM is the ease of configuration, integrations and customizations. The configurations are simply click and drag, and can be self-service. Because Microsoft Dynamic

CRM is written in SQL, integrations and customizations are much easier. Reporting of data for ownership and management is now on demand and no longer has to be requested from someone else. Live data dashboards, rather than a requested report, are truly useful. By the time a requested report is generated, most of the time the relevance of the information has passed.

The Outlook App for the smartphone gives you all your email, calendar and contacts just like your desktop. To me, it seems some of the other apps are not as useful with having to jump from one app to another because the calendar is in one app, contacts in another and email in a third.

Office Products – Work, Excel, PowerPoint, etc. all have apps for your smart device that give you the full resources of the desktop.

Having all of my office tools on my smartphone and tablet means I can work anywhere. I remember the days of having to update everything back at the office. What a waste of time. My wife has a rule on dealing with tasks - - "Touch it once." Imagine getting a call for a client who just got around to reading your proposal. You can instantly create a Skype call and track the activity in your CRM. Share your screen with your prospect to review the proposal and update as you go, if needed, save the update and email the pdf to the prospect while tracking everything in CRM with notes of the meeting included. Other team members can be brought into the call if needed. Following the rule of "touch it once," is achievable when using your smart device apps as you go about your everyday tasks without being burdened by trying to remember what is next.

Shopping

Why on earth would I include shopping is a business book? All of us can get distracted with having to run by the store to pick things up on the way home, over lunch or even during the day. There are several tools that can help with that and reduce the amount of time taken out of your day. Let's look at four different tools:

> Smart Phone apps such as Grocery IQ or Out of Milk can help you keep track of what you need to buy and minimize your time in the stores.

Sam's Club Scan & Go app for your smart phone can help you get out of the store faster by using your phone to scan items as you place them in your shopping cart. Once you have completed shopping, you go to the front of the store, press Pay on your app, and it processes the purchases. You walk out of the store, without having to stand in the checkout line.

Amazon, Amazon Prime and Amazon Prime Now keep you out of the store and deliver to your house or business. Prime is an annual subscription that provides two-day shipping at no additional cost on most items. Prime Now delivers to your house within two hours. How many times have you been involved in a project and realized that you needed something to complete the job? With Prime Now, you just order the item online, they bring it to you, and you save time—time spent getting ready to go to the store, time spent driving to and from the store and time trying to find what you need at the store, not to mention saving money by not finding another thing you see at the store because you didn't have to go there in the first place. There are other online merchants who deliver free if you spend X dollars.

The fourth tool keeps you out of the store, but you do have to drive by the store. Walmart, Kroger and many other stores have online pick up. Just order online, drive to the pickup section in the parking lot at the store and call the number to let them know you have arrived. They bring the items out and load them into your car.

As we work on becoming A Super Hero, we'll re-establish our work/life balance, become better employees/business owners and better rounded individuals. It is time to take charge of our day. **A Super Hero leverages technology to over-achieve,** to perform research, and to seek knowledge. Therefore, join me in the Becoming a Super Hero Movement.

––––

Thom Coats

Thom is a business developer whose entrepreneurial instincts and clear vision have assisted in the growth of multiple companies.

Thom stands at the forefront of the solutions-based technology industry. Thom has 25 years of experience in new business development, serving roles from sales to district manager to Vice President of Sales with corporations such as Century II, Paychex, and NFIB.

Thom has been strategically positioned at the JourneyTEAM of Nashville as the Vice President of Sales. Here, he is responsible for building new business in the southeast US region for mid-size to large companies through the use of Microsoft Dynamics and SharePoint business solution applications and NCR software. Thom enjoys helping his clients succeed by implementing solutions that work.

Thom's father had a motto --"You can only sell what you have faith in!" At JourneyTEAM, Thom exhibits passion for the product -- productive, profitable clients who can focus on their business rather than the systems they support! His efforts enable businesses to implement solutions that increase efficiency within their workflow. He believes that his position at JourneyTEAM is the culmination of all of his life and work experiences.

With an array of interests and affiliations, Thom stays connected to the community through investing time and energy on the Advisory Board for the Murfreesboro Youth Orchestra, and Read to Succeed. In 2014, he was honored as the Read to Succeed Council Member of the Year. Thom also exercised his desire to give back as a police officer of 6 years -- a position that molded him to be an excellent communicator. During his time on the force, he focused on Crime Prevention and Child Safety Programs.

Thom is a Partner of Accelerent as well as host of the Technology Subgroup, and is Vice President of Southeast Business Forum. He is an active participant in the Walter Hill church of Christ. He and his wife Judy have 3 sons, and 2 daughters-in-law.

Thom is a third generation entrepreneur, which gives him great insight in understanding what clients want and need. His grandfather's Bible is displayed in his office helps him never forget who he is, and where he came from.

7

Moving Your Team's Performance From Stuck to Unstuck

Regardless of your service or product, your people (employees) are the key to deliver them. But let's face it, sometimes your team gets "stuck" in some way. Your latest hire is not producing as anticipated. Your team is not working cohesively as you expected. You are simply frustrated because success isn't occurring at the rate or pace you projected. Whatever the reason, your team is STUCK.

Over time, this negative pull is difficult to overcome for both the team and the leader.

In this chapter, we will explore leadership skills that create clarity and sustainability with your team. Despite the aspect your team finds itself stuck, these practical tips will ignite their creative spark to find a productive solution.

Creating Momentum

It is tough to win a game when no one knows the rules. The same is true for your team. All too often, we assume our employees know what is expected of them. After all, good performance is a matter of common sense, right? Well, it's not, and neither are the details of your expectations.

Most of the time, poor employee performance issues stem from the false assumption of clear expectations when, in fact, a shared understanding is not in place. As leaders, we assume our expectations were clearly communicated, but there is a disconnect—a "fuzzy" understanding of exactly what you expect compared to employees' perception of what you expect. Due to this disconnect, performance isn't where it should be, and it becomes difficult for leaders to initiate conversation that guides employees back on track.

Consider this practical strategy—spend time clarifying expectations with current employees. Take assumption out of the equation. Ensure every person on the team understands two key requirements of their job: 1) WHAT needs to be done—functional aspects of the job (product knowledge, sales goals, deliverables, how to operate a machine, etc.), and 2) HOW the job needs to be done—relational parts of the job (how to communicate with customers, what follow-through looks like, how to take initiative on tasks, needs, etc.) Any aspect of positive job performance includes both tactical and relational elements which means job expectations should as well. When ground rules (expectations) are clarified up front, the necessary feedback conversation that may occur down the road has a reference point which helps create necessary movement toward the desired performance.

Consider this example: Leaders often fall short of clarity because they falsely assume a shared meaning has been created with their employee. Leaders may say the same words, but two different interpretations exist. For example, "I want you to be a team player!" is the instruction. Leaders expect employees to display behavior such as initiative, follow-up, anticipating needs, and offering their assistance. But employees hear, "Do your job." Both nod their heads in agreement of understanding; in fact, leaders may ask employees if they understand the instructions (they say "yes", by the way). However, employee performance doesn't measure up to expectations. Leaders become frustrated and give negative feedback to their employees. In turn, employees are frustrated, assuming they were doing what was asked of them. The result? Employees are stuck in poor performance and don't think they are, and leaders are stuck trying to help employees understand their expectations.

Another challenge leaders face has to do with employees who perform well on one spectrum yet lack performance in another. For example, you may have an employee who is technically competent with inventory processes (the WHAT), but he is rude to co-workers (the HOW). Or, perhaps an employee is very helpful to customers (HOW), but lacks technical computer skills (WHAT). Effective performance includes both aspects of tactical and relational skills. Employees must have both to be successful and equally important in setting expectations.

To close this gap, consider two specific steps:

1. Use as many examples as possible when communicating expectations. Describe the expectation in terms of tangible language

employees can experience in some way. For example, initiative means asking other members of the team how you can help them when you finish your work early. Don't leave it to chance for your employee to figure out what you mean.

2. Ask employees to tell you (not repeat back) their understanding of stated expectations. As they began to describe what they heard, you (the manager or team leader) can determine if shared understanding has taken place. If not, continue the dialogue with additional examples until a shared meaning exists.

Your team's performance hinges on this first step. In fact, it's likely the root cause of an employee's performance deficiency. Start here. If you have a "stuck" employee, this conversation will set the stage for future conversations to get them back on track. We'll tackle those feedback conversations in the next section.

Sustaining Momentum

Congratulations! Once your team understands expectations and is performing at a desired level, the team is on the right track for success. But wait...your job of leadership isn't over yet. Creating momentum in performance requires maintenance and, in the workplace, it requires follow-up and attention by both you (the leader) and each team member. This section of the chapter highlights actions leaders can take that will sustain momentum initiated by setting clear expectations.

Leaders often believe they communicate clearly with their teams. However, employees are not mind readers, even those you have worked with you for a long time. Constructive feedback is hard for anyone to hear. While your words may be intended to help employees get back on track, if they don't perceive those words as helpful, your message will never be heard. You have two goals in performance feedback: 1) employees need to keep an open mind during your conversation (reducing a defensive response), and 2) employees understand your message so the desired change in behavior can occur (can they see the gap in performance as you do?). For this to occur, employees must be empowered to trust you. They must believe you have their (and the team's) best interest at heart, especially during those tough conversations. Be intentional with your approachability, clarity, and consistency so those tougher conversations can occur. When this happens, those feedback conversations will create movement.

What can you do when an employee's performance has declined? As a leader or manager, you notice a trend in negative behavior occurring (without self-improvement) and you feel the need to address it. Consider using this analogy: WD-40 and duct tape are tactical solutions to repair household issues and their principles apply to human behavior, too.

Use the concept of WD-40 to "un-stick" behaviors that impede your team's success. Humans, by nature, are prone to slip into unproductive habits. We value routine and, let's face it, over time, poor behavior sneaks in and becomes the norm. Negative habits can be anything from habitual tardiness to missed deadlines. So, what is the WD-40 weapon designed to address negative behavior and enact change? It's your feedback! Integrate quick weekly check-ins with every person. Get updates on deadlines, co-worker dynamics, and needs/wants from management. After all, it's much easier to stop a bad habit before it starts.

The concept of duct tape secures behaviors that help teams achieve success. There is a powerful dynamic at play when each team member shows up and does their part toward a goal. More is accomplished and momentum builds, positively impacting your team's energy and engagement. Leaders, be the duct tape and ensure your team comes together on a regular basis (in person or virtually). Talk about what is working and not working within the team. Most important, give them what they need from you—information, time, removing barriers, etc.—to sustain momentum.

There is one last note to mention for leaders—to act efficiently, we sometimes store up our feedback and deliver several messages at once. The conversation happens when addressing a specific performance concern, but in our misguided attempt for efficiency, we say something like, "By the way, while we're together, here's one more thing I'd like to discuss with you." Sounds Innocent enough, right? We assume this is a smart use of our time to address one more thing, but the employee mentally shuts down. Why? We've been living with this negative performance feedback for a while. We've been observing behavior and silently contemplating dialogue with our employee(s). However, they are hearing our message for the first time, trying to make sense of the performance problem brought to their attention. The second feedback message is communicated but, in most cases, the behavior doesn't improve the way we hoped. We mean well (and that's good), but our employees feel like negative grenades are coming at them with every additional comment.

Keep it simple. Provide constructive feedback on one action item at a time so employees don't run and take cover every time you need to chat with them for a few minutes.

I encourage you to visit your nearest hardware store and buy a can of WD-40 and a roll of duct tape. These two items serve as a great reminder to me and will help you remember the important concepts of removing negative employee performance and promoting greater team collaboration.

Once clear performance expectations are in place, the leader's ability to provide honest, timely, and clear coaching feedback to employees is the secret to initiate necessary momentum when employees are stuck. While difficult decisions are sometimes required, in most situations, your feedback is the tool that ignites and energizes the team. And when that happens, your employees become unstuck!

The Leader's Challenge

Finally, let's spend some time focusing on you, the leader. Leading and managing people is tough. In fact, I'm convinced if most of us knew how difficult the job would be, we may not have taken it. Yet at the same time, leading others can be tremendously rewarding when a breakthrough occurs and results begin to appear on an individual and team level. Great leaders never assume the team's momentum will continue without their focus. In this last segment, we will focus on three skills to cultivate as a leader that will challenge and inspire your team to continued greatness.

We will start with perspective. As leaders, we often forget that employees have a different mindset than we do. Your view of the organization includes budgets, forecasts, and strategy; your employees' perspectives are often much different. They don't think about or see the same information you do which means their viewpoint is much more limited. Your employee deals with his daily work schedule and customers x, y, and z which represents a tactical and here-and-now mindset. A wise leader translates information into their employees' language to connect the day-to-day perspective to a broader one. For example, how does a decision to reduce spending on certain office supplies make sense to employees when they believe said supplies are necessary to do their jobs? Or how can you help employees understand a particular policy that, on the surface, may seem to add steps to a process but ultimately protects the company? The ability to connect the dots helps employees better understand your business decisions. When there is a lack of understanding on those *why* concepts, employees get stuck in their thinking, falsely believing they know more about the business than you do. This extra step of communication yields trust and engagement for you.

In addition to respecting your perspective differences, your team needs to know the objectives they are working toward. They may be called many things: vision, direction, strategy, etc., so when possible, go beyond the day-to-day operations and let your team know the next three to six months' projected goals. What new customers or accounts are you pursuing? Is there a new product or service under review? Where do you see the revenues and profits of the team in the next few months, and what will those profits mean to the team? Creating clarity is a critical business skill, and anything short of that allows assumptions to enter your employees' minds. In today's fast-paced and competitive marketplace, no business can afford a team that is almost meeting their goals. Without this information, complacency and routine set in. Employees show up for the eight hours they must give in exchange for a paycheck. Over time, that routine may produce a "well, that's good enough" mindset which leads to those STUCK behaviors we try to prevent. Show your team the potential future. Employees naturally want to be a part of something bigger than themselves. This vision-casting skill creates energy across your organization, even amid trying circumstances.

Accountability is the second skill leaders must make a priority to ensure unproductive behaviors don't influence the team. Every member of your team must be responsible for their performance. They have an opportunity to be rewarded for success or face the consequences based on poor task performance.

An accountable mindset means leaders must be willing to address poor performing employees, particularly those with chronic issues. We discussed the importance of providing performance feedback earlier in the chapter, however, leaders sometimes struggle with mustering the courage to have tough conversations with poor performing employees, especially those who have worked with you for a long period of time. Performance improves slightly with your corrective feedback then declines again in a repetitive cycle. The destructive nature of this pattern negatively impacts the rest of the team.

Consider this example with an employee named Larry. His co-workers say things like, "Well, that's just Larry. He's been here ten years. You will get used to him; we have." Or they say, "I can't believe our manager doesn't see how Larry does just enough to get by. It doesn't seem fair." The longer Larry remains on the team, the more your leadership reputation suffers. Over time, other employees' performance will often decline. They tire of filling in for Larry's deficiencies and their desire to give you 100% wanes. As Larry's leader, be honest with him about his poor performance. Give him specific examples of areas that require focus and create an improvement plan that is monitored over a set period of time. If his performance remains insufficient, you must make the difficult decision on the next steps. If not, your entire time will eventually suffer.

Finally, don't miss the opportunity to focus on your own development. This third priority area is the critical distinction of leaders who achieve stellar results. Craig Groeschel, senior pastor at LifeChurch sums it up well, "Everyone wins when the leader gets better." He's right, but finding the time to get better must be intentional. Leaders are busy, and focusing on personal development often takes a backseat to many other demands. I encourage you to be selfish. Invest in yourself. You will become more effective and so will your team.

The many demands of your role often push any personal development to the back burner. While your intent may be present, the reality of life will continually delay plans you may have for yourself. Consider adding a monthly appointment to your calendar that motivates you to reflect on the previous thirty days. Identify intentional learning events, progress made to your goals, and future plans. The hour spent in reflection maintains the priority of your development.

Parents often warn their children to be mindful of keeping good company, and so it is with leaders in the workplace. Make it a point to identify someone in your circle of influence who you can learn from. Leadership can be lonely especially if you are the business owner. You need someone you can be vulnerable with, a sounding board for concerns or questions, and someone you can learn from. Who do you know in your immediate circle that you admire for their experience, accomplishments, or expertise? Spend time with them and get to know them on a personal level. This informal mentoring helps you grow, but can also ensure you don't get stuck. If the leader is stuck, it is impossible for the team not to be too.

I have often heard it said that there is no such thing as no influence. You are either moving things forward or backward. A standstill cannot exist. So, ask yourself, how am I moving my team or organization forward? Are we making progress because of my efforts? Am I a roadblock to advancement in some way? The focus you place on personal leadership development impacts those outcomes.

There are many traps that can impact the people side of your business, both for your team as well as you the leader. Those traps can get us stuck in some way. If you do your best to clearly communicate expectations, provide consistent meaningful feedback, and stay focused on your own development, your team is poised to achieve great results.
So, where do you begin? One action today starts that journey. And yes, you can help your people get unstuck one step at a time.

8

Making Connections

I make connections for a living.

As a software engineer, as the assistant director of a ministry, as the editor of a magazine, as a speaker, and as a writer, my job is to connect the dots.

I bet that's your job, too.

Educational philosophy tells us there are three stages—called the Trivium—to learning:

Grammar, Dialectic, and Rhetoric. The Bible calls these states Knowledge, Understanding, and Wisdom.

It goes like this.

Grammar involves terminology, the building blocks of learning a subject, whether it's reading, writing, or arithmetic; rocket science or brain surgery; music, art, or poetry; parenting, software engineering, or deep sea diving. There's a common vocabulary and vernacular to any field of study and endeavor that must first be learned before the next stage can be attempted.

The dialectic stage is where the student begins to wrestle with ideas built on the grammar of the subject. *Does this mean what I think it means? If X is true, is Y also true?* It's where we argue and challenge assumptions to make sure every coin drops into the proper chute, every idea balances on its respective premise.

Once this framework has been built and tested, its truths and truisms can be applied to ideas, thought patterns, and problems to create new solutions. Here we've entered the rhetoric phase, the wisdom phase. It's where we make connections between the things we've learned and apply them in a new way to solve a new problem, extrapolating and interpolating from disparate experiences to resolve a crisis.

This is where we connect the dots.

This is why you—out of all candidates—were hired for that job, why you—out of all RFPs— landed that contract, why you—out of all your family, friends, and classmates—started the business you did. You excelled at connecting the dots, applying knowledge and understanding to the hand you were dealt, and did what was wise.

And though your daily bread requires you to make connections, you may find yourself struggling with one particular kind of connecting: with people.

Connecting to the Right People

Let's face it, business runs on people.
Families run on people. Churches, charities, governments; architecture, the fashion industry, the food supply—providing our basic needs in Maslow's Hierarchy: food, clothing, and shelter—all run on people.
In the same way *you* were chosen for the job or the contract or the business, there are specific people that excel in each area of our lives, business or otherwise.

That's why connecting with others is so important.

Even if you're not a connector by nature, you can learn to make the connections you need to break through to your next growth phase.

Being a Connector

There are two types of connecting: face-to-face and through technology.

Whenever you have the opportunity to network, introduce yourself. Not to everyone. To one person.

Ask, "What do you do?" "Tell me about you." "What brings you here?" Open-ended questions tell you a lot. Ask, then shut up and listen.

You don't have to "work a room" if you're not comfortable doing that. Don't be a business card collector. Be a connector connector. Look for opportunities to introduce your new friend to another friend. If you're not going to follow-up within 24 hours, throw the business card away.

Those I've "met" only electronically, I have adopted a "Coffee, Lunch, or Beer" policy, by which I do my best to meet in person, as well. But still, technological connections are worth pursuing even if an in-real-life meeting never takes place.

This is the essence of Twitter, really: a constant stream of conversation speeding past 24/7. You jump in, you post your 140 characters, then you jump out. It's hard to participate in that stream, BUT it is a very effect way to reach out to others in a non-threatening, non-committal way, to get a conversation going.

Periscope is another venue you can use to connect, both as a broadcaster and as a viewer. Because Periscope handles typically match up with Twitter handles, you can usually take the conversation off-broadcast and continue it on Twitter. The same is true of Facebook Live and other live-streaming platforms.

Networking and connecting overlap, but they are two very different activities. Networking is finding people who can help you. Connecting is about finding ways to help others, usually by finding someone else who can help.

The Right Connections

In business, there are three kinds of people you want to connect with: Colleagues/Friends,

Vendors, and Customers. This is what is known as the Referral Triangle.

The Referral Triangle

Colleagues/Friend

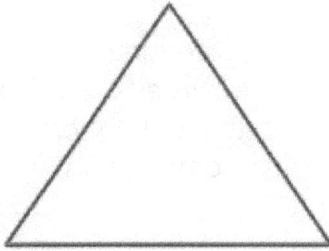

Vendors   Customers

Colleagues/Friends – These are the folks you do life with. The ones who work at your company, go to your church, serve on your board, live in your neighborhood, bowl in your league, exercise at your gym.

Vendors – You buy from these people, because they provide goods and/or services you need.

Customers – You sell to these people, because you provide goods and/or services they need.

Of course, all of these people can overlap. But I want you to consider them as separate groups for our purposes, because you're going to look in different places for colleagues/friends than you would for vendors; and you'll look for customers in different places still.

That said, when it comes down to it, they're people and the precepts for connecting with people are the same, regardless of where they fall on this triangle.

Being a Connector

There are as many different reasons to connect as there are people to connect with. And you won't be able to make a strong connection with everyone you meet.

You just won't.

When looking to make a connection, ask yourself three questions:

1. What is my reason for connecting?
2. What is their reason for connecting?
3. What action do I want my new connection to take?

My Reason

Before you make plans to connect, decide WHY you want to connect. There is no wrong *why*, but the *why* will determine the *who* and the *how*. So be honest with yourself on why you want to connect. Here's a non-exhaustive list of reasons you might be looking to connect with others.

Friends. Are you new to your area, to your field of work, to your stage of life? Finding friends to do life with is a common reason to connect with others. Finding similar interests in entertainment, activities, hobbies, life philosophy, vocation, ministry, missions, etc., help us not to feel alone in a world of seven billion people.

Colleagues. Folks making strides in the same area; solving the same issues; working in similar industries. Or doing similar functions in disparate industries.

Sales. It's really OK to want to make sales. And you have to connect with people to do it.

Right People. In life, we often need others to walk along with us, to share the burden; or to bring their genius to an area where we lack. Whether you're looking for a new employee, service provider, mentor, coach, sponsor, or life partner, you need to know what you're looking for.

Be a Resource. Maybe you're on the giving end. You "know a guy" who can do most anything. You're the maven people go to when they're looking to make a connection.

Your reason for connecting can be any or all or a subset of the above. The key is to *know* why you're connecting and be able to articulate it, at least to yourself.

Their Reason

Just like you might have a myriad of reasons to connect, so does the person you want to connect with. God gave you two ears and one mouth; listen twice as much as you speak, and hear their reason for connecting. It might not match up with yours, but that's OK. Adjust and offer what you can. In all cases, be honest with them and you about your *why*s. If the connection isn't there, acknowledge it and move on.

Call to Action

It's important to ask your new connection, *What can I do for you?* or *How can I help you? Who would be a good introduction for you?* But be ready with your own answer to those questions.

Do you want to be referred? Do you want to refer someone to them? Or refer them to someone? Are you looking for a referral?

Do you want them to buy from you? Do you want to buy from them?

Do you want them to accept your invitation to an event? Do you want to be invited to an event?

Know ahead of time what you want them to do and don't leave the encounter without a Yes, No, or next appointment. If it's the last one, be sure to follow up!

Events

Not all events are created equal. Sometimes "networking" events are not the best places to make connections. On the other hand, if you're prepared, you can make connections anywhere, whether it's the school pick-up line, the dry cleaners, the coffee shop, at a restaurant, a conference, or an arena event.

That said, events can be a great place to connect, but you have to be intentional.

Be Present

The first law of connecting is to be present. Go to events, go to meet-ups, go to Toastmasters meetings, go to the coffee shop, go to sporting events, go when your colleagues invite you, and find things to do where you can invite others. But whatever you do…

Go.

Go early. Allow margin on either end of the event for connecting. You can go early, or stay late. Or both.

If you are able to show up early, volunteer. Work the registration table. Help set up. Stand at the door and greet arrivals. Offer directions to key areas: food, drinks, restrooms, presentation spaces, vendor hall, etc.

If you are able to stay late, offer to clean up, help break down, help vendors pack up, collect lost articles. Alternately, have a scheduled or impromptu one-on-one with a fellow attendee or vendor to strengthen the connection.

One connector makes a point of helping clean up at networking events. When the announcement made that the event is over and "please clean up around you," he makes the rounds to take the trash from people's hands, so their hands and minds are free for making connections. Connecting is about removing barriers to collaboration.

Before You Go

Even if you have an email list and use a service like Emma or Click Dimensions, Mail Chimp or Constant Contact, send personal invites to colleague with whom you have a strong rapport. Or would like to build one. A person email or phone call will go a long way toward strengthening that relationship, and toward encouraging your connection to attend.

If possible, plan to meet one or more of your guests before the event to plan your connection strategy: Who do you want to meet? Who do you want to strengthen a connection with? What are you hoping to accomplish at this event? Talk it beforehand and know what you're each going.

Plan to meet afterward to debrief, share connections, share notes, and strengthen your own connection.

Don't Go Alone

- Take a friend – Bring a guest to an event they may not have access to, or might not know about it. Bring a guest so that you know someone else at the event and the two of you can be strategic about meeting as many new people as possible. That way, if you get stuck with someone who is dominating your time, you can rescue one another, or at the very least know that other connections are happening for you while you're tied up.
- Take a dish – If the event calls for it, bring a dish that you would like to eat or drink. If possible, make it memorable.

- Take your business cards – But don't just hand them out frivolously. You paid good money for those cards; hand them out to people who will respect them, who will you them to call you, connect you, and refer you.
- Take your appointment calendar – Even if it's on your smart phone, be ready to set follow-up appointments on the spot and know when you're available. Some circumstances may make sense for you to plan ahead of time an appointment schedule to follow-up with people you're meeting. Especially if your event is out of town and your access to attendees is limited. If you are traveling for the event, can you arrive early or stay late and plan appointments during those buffers around the event?
- Take your smile, your warm handshake, and your willingness to help.

After You Go

Follow up:

- with your friend to compare notes
     Who did you meet? Who do you need to follow-up with? Did you learn of any opportunities for your company? Did you learn any other networking events? Did you gain any

intelligence that could help either of you in the future?

- with your connections for your next appointment

    Did you set a follow-up appointment? Make sure it's in your calendar. Do you need to set a follow-up appointment? Do it right way.

- with introductions you promised to make

    Determine if the introduction is best made via phone, email, or in person; then make it happen.

- with invitations to other relevant events

    If you know of other gatherings that your new connections should know about, get it on their calendar now by sending out the invite. If you can attend as well, invite them to be your guest. If you can't attend, make an introduction for them beforehand with someone who will be so they don't go in alone.

Event Pro-tips:

- Don't eat. Unless it's a sit-down dinner and you can use that time to meet new people. You'll also then have your hands free to shake hands, and hand out business cards.

- Stand between the door and bar/food: the high traffic areas, but not in such a way as to cause a traffic jam.

  I was once attending an event that had a coffee machine in a prominent place for the day-to-day use of its patrons. For this event, though, coffee had been brought in in air pot dispensers, so a sign had been placed on the coffee machine to not use it. The air pots were placed on a low table and difficult to see through the crowd. To the dismay of many early-morning attendees who made a bee-line to the coffee machine; their hopes were dashed by the sign. I stood near the machine, cup in hand, and was the hero to several of them when I told them where the fresh, hot coffee could be found. With the ice broken, conversation was much easier and I made several new connections that day.

- Don't talk to your friends (except to introduce them) … you can catch up with them anytime. This isn't party time, it's business time. Use it wisely and strategically to find someone you can help. Any bit of time you are talking with a friend, open up your "circle" to make an opening for others to come join the discussion. Let people see you together, but then separate to meet new people.

- Ask for a business card (or if you can connect via LinkedIn) AFTER a connection has been made. Make sure there's a reason to talk again before asking for a way to make it happen.

  When you have been given a business card (or a LinkedIn Profile), READ the card or profile before you go any further; use it as a conversation-starter. All of the information conveyed before is led to this sharing of information; take it seriously, take interest in this new information and discuss it. If needed, take notes on the card.

- Don't sell at an event (unless you've paid for a booth and are standing at it); GIVE something away: a lead, a referral, an invitation.

- Don't walk away until you have a YES, NO, or have set a follow-up appointment

Online Connections

Making connections online through social media or via email can be just as effective as face-to-face meetings... sometimes more so. But the norms and mores are different, even though you're connecting with the same people.

For one thing, 93% of communication in person is non-verbal. In email, that 93% is owned by the reader. Their day is coming to forefront of their mind as they "hear" you speak your email.

That's why it's very important to establish the tone of your communication at the outset.

If you just had a great face-to-face meeting, tell them how great it was to see/meet/talk to them at XYZ Event. Put them back into the comradery of your last conversation, before going on to your reason for emailing. If it's been awhile since that connection conversation, open with encouraging well-wishes: "Happy Monday, I hope this week is off to a good start for you," "Happy New Year! May you have an epic 2017," etc. If you know something personal you can inquire about, do it: a project, a recent trip, inquire after a family member. The goal is to get them back to remembering your smile, your warm handshake, your willingness to help.

Using LinkedIn

LinkedIn is a platform for connecting with your colleagues, your prospects, your industry influencers, your neighbors, your family, your friend from third grade, etc., all on a professional level.

When LinkedIn first started, it seemed like a sort of "Facebook for Business" and Monster combined. It was where you basically posted your resume by listing all of the places you have worked under *Experience*, and listing bullet points of what you did there. While that may have some merit when you're looking for a job, it's not the best use of the space when you are looking for new business, new connections, and new referrals.

Setting up your profile

Your profile is about you... but only insomuch as it communicates how you can help the reader. John Nemo, creator of LinkedIn Riches, suggests a straight-forward, 7-fold message your Summary and current Role should deliver: 1) what you do, 2) who you do it for, 3) why it works, 4) what makes you different, 5) what others say about you, 6) how it works, and 7) how to get started.

I highly recommend you get his free template and simply fill in the blanks for the business connection you're trying to make:
https://linkedinriches.com/summary/

In addition to all of the regular content areas where you describe what problems you solve for your clients, be sure to include as much about you as you can that will help people break the ice with you. The goal here is to make yourself approachable; you want them to *contact you*.

Include your school and what you did there. If there's something specifically poignant about your alma mater that will be a good conversation started, add it. Add your publications, awards, association memberships, presentation slides, and projects you're doing with others. The more information you can include about you as a person, rather than you as a resume, the more connection points you will find with others.

Profile picture

Be sure your headshot shows you as you are. If you spend any of your time meeting new people at events, for coffee, etc., they need to be able to recognize you when you walk in the door.

If your hair changes (shorter, longer, different color, shaved; and that goes for facial hair, too, gentlemen), if you wear glasses now (or got rid of them because you had Lazik), be sure to update your headshot. And make sure it's no more than two years old.

People you meet in person first, need to be sure you're the person they just met; people you meet online need to recognize you when they meet you in person. Which also means your profile picture should be of your face, and only your face: no logos, no group shots, no full-body shots. Your connections want to connect with YOU. Make it easy for them to be sure it *is* you.

Sending Invitations

LinkedIn is built on invitations to connect. They help you out with some templated phrases.

Don't use them.

You are making personal connections; make your invitation personal. Tell them why you want to connect. Be sure to make it about them.

The same goes for congratulating people on new jobs and work anniversaries; personalize the greeting, don't just accept the standard.

Searches

If you are looking to grow your network in a specific city, use Advanced Search (look for the small link to the right of the search box) and filter by your city. For warm referrals, look for people who are you 2nd Connections. Then reach out to your shared connections and ask for a real warm introduction; face-to-face, if possible.

Here's a tip for growing your reach. Do a search for the Title of a person you want to meet; limit it to 2nd Degree connections in your city. Then save that search (look for the link on the top left of the search results, next to the gear). Every week (from the moment you save it), LinkedIn will send you an email with NEW connections that meet that criteria.

That means, you'll be notified weekly when someone in your network moves to your city, takes a new job with the title you're looking for and/or just moved from 3rd degree or higher to 2nd, because you added a new connection OR one of your connections did.

Think about that.

You'll get an email EACH week of new people to connect with, to whom you can ask for a warm introduction from someone you already know.

Job searches can be another way to find people. If you are a software consultant, you can find companies that use your software by looking for job postings that require proficiency or familiarity with that software. Once you find the company; you can see all of the 2nd degree people you know who work there.

Surely one of them would be a good connection for you. Or could introduce you to one.

People Make the World Go 'Round

Whether you're connecting in person or online or both, remember to be:

- Client-focused
- Warm and inviting
- Great at following-up
- Giving of yourself

These simple steps will help you move beyond collecting business cards.

They will help start collecting friends...and a personal sales team!

9

Getting Unstuck – The Competitive Advantage of OC

"Culture Eats Strategy for Lunch" ~ Peter Drucker

The Missing Piece

Talk to anyone who's been in business for more than a minute and they will tell you successful organizations have two common components: 1) great leadership, and 2) a winning business strategy. But extraordinary organizations have a third, often hidden component, one that most leaders either take for granted or overlook completely—a positive, winning Organizational Culture (OC). Time and time again, it's proven that OC creates an impenetrable competitive advantage for those that unlock its secrets.

The world has changed and today employees are looking at organizations differently. They don't simply want a job or even a career—they want an experience. According to Deloitte in a 2016 survey, 95% of job candidates believe OC is more important than compensation and less than 5% of candidates value compensation over OC. But what exactly is OC?

What is Organizational Culture (OC)?

An organization's culture (OC) is like a country's culture. It's the shared traditions, beliefs, values, philosophies, and actions of the people who make up the organization. In other words, quite simply, it's *how things get done*, the way employees think and act, and what forms the basis of their decisions at work.

All organizations have an OC. The question for leaders is, "Is it helping or hurting your organization?" Many people mistakenly believe OC is only about a positive culture, but the fact is, ALL organizations have an OC and some OCs are toxic and negative leading to dysfunction which limits performance.

Unlocking the Secret to a Compelling OC

Figuring out your Organizational Culture (OC) isn't hard. In fact, it's incredibly simple if you can stomach the truth. **The OC Equation™**, like the theory of relativity, provides a clear roadmap that you can actually understand and use to not only diagnose your organizational culture (OC) but figure out practical, effective changes to improve it and get results. But beware; beneath **The OC Equation's™** simplicity lies a rabbit hole into values, philosophies, systems and processes, policies and procedures, and internal and external actions. Its significance doesn't pave the way for the creation of a physical bomb, but it does pave the way for an organizational bomb that can, by its sheer strength and power, infiltrate every cranny of your organization.

When the components of **The OC Equation™** are consistently applied and leveraged as a key business strategy, they can change the face and dynamics of your organization which allows you to attract and retain top talent and inspire performance. Employees will be perpetually engaged, deliver high performance, and make decisions as if they owned the company. Organizational Culture can create a sustainable, truly proprietary competitive advantage for your organization that competitors can't duplicate.

Using a simple, but powerful equation—**The OC Equation™**—you can discover what makes up your current OC, deterine if it aligns with and supports what your organization says it values, and if it's inspiring and engaging your talent. Once you've identified your current OC, you can begin evaluating its effectiveness. Does it engage employees and empower them to get results and go the extra mile? If not, the second half of the book will provide a roadmap for putting together a workable action plan to unleash your employees' passion, potential, and performance and create the one true competitive advantage.

The OC Equation™

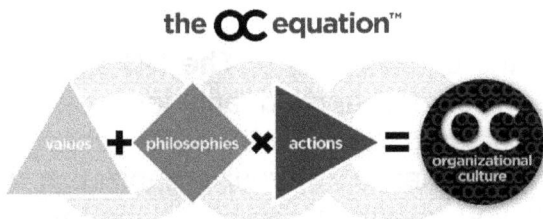

the **OC** equation™

values + philosophies × actions = **OC** organizational culture

Building a Strong Organizational Culture (OC)

The importance and impact of OC can't be overemphasized. It's the "secret sauce" of your competitive advantage both internally in attracting and retaining top talent and externally with providing uncompromising service to your customers. However, few leaders have the vision and tenacity to grasp it as an integral part of their overall business strategy.

What would your reaction be if I told you I had the equivalent of the next iPod©, Post-It Note© or even the next Google© in your industry and that, if implemented, revenue and profits were expected to be triple that of your current products or services? Most leaders would say "WOW—I'd like a piece of that action!" And, like me, they would probably begin immediately looking for ways to capitalize on and integrate it into their strategic business model.

Why is it then that highly competent, seasoned leaders constantly overlook the power of an intentional organizational culture (OC) when developing and implementing their overall business strategy? Quite often it seems much easier to develop new products or services than to deal with those dreaded "people" issues. As a matter of fact, most leaders hire people and then forget about them unless, of course, they do something so egregious they need to be fired—and then, they assume that HR or someone else will handle that too.

Why Care About OC?

Recently a business colleague said:

> *"To be perfectly honest, I am ambivalent about this subject [OC] because I feel that most HR people concentrate far too much of their time and effort just talking, and talking, and talking some more about this subject, even though a company's culture is important to recruitment and, most importantly, retention. What line management cannot understand is why HR likes to talk incessantly about culture and other conceptual issues, thereby avoiding the real hard BUSINESS issues that they face every day. While I fully recognize the value of having a well-defined, people-oriented culture, in my view, HR would gain a lot more respect from line management if: a) It would take the time to define the culture of THEIR COMPANY, rather than a "wanna be" culture, b) get management's approval, publish it, and train all management on its content, c) cease all the unnecessary talk about the culture, and d) start to*

help line management achieve its BUSINESS objectives by utilizing various HR services."

This comment helped me realize that many business leaders (including HR business leaders) don't fully understand the competitive advantage lying at their fingertips, often untapped and grossly underutilized, waiting to be discovered, harnessed, and cultivated as their one true competitive advantage—their OC. So, the question becomes—WHY? Why should I give a hoot about this thing called OC (Organizational Culture)? The answer is simple—revenue and profits!

Most leaders, at least the effective ones, make decisions based on data. Most want to see hard facts and details and take the time to mull them over carefully before jumping into a decision. To that end, let's explore validated research linking business performance and results to employee engagement and, ultimately, organizational culture (OC). Simply stated, when employees feel connected to the organization, they become actively engaged, meaning they are willing to expend discretionary effort to make things happen. The Conference Board defines employee engagement as *"A heightened emotional and intellectual Connection that an employee has for his/her job, organization, manager or co-*

workers, that influences him/her to apply additional discretionary effort to his/her work."

Connections are made when employees feel like they belong and are comfortable with the organization's values, philosophies, and how those are expressed through consistent, predictable actions that support those values and philosophies creating the OC.

OC = Employee Engagement = Business Results

"A great (organizational) culture (OC) will outperform a mediocre culture", says Dave Logan, author of *Tribal Leadership*. While most of us intuitively accept that an organization's culture (OC) is important, many business leaders dismiss it as a "touchy-feely" management buzz word, not worthy of an active role in the overall business strategic planning process.

Now you may be thinking, why are we talking about employee engagement? I thought we were talking about organizational culture (OC). The fact of the matter is that employee engagement, the amount of discretionary effort an employee is willing to exert on behalf of their organization, is a result of the employee's level of engagement.

Through their groundbreaking research, Gallup has repeatedly demonstrated that companies with highly engaged workforces outperform their peers by 147% in earnings per share and realize:

- 41% fewer quality defects
- 48% fewer safety incidents
- 28% less shrinkage
- 65% less turnover (low-turnover organizations)
- 25% less turnover (high-turnover organizations)
- 37% less absenteeism

(Gallup, 2012)

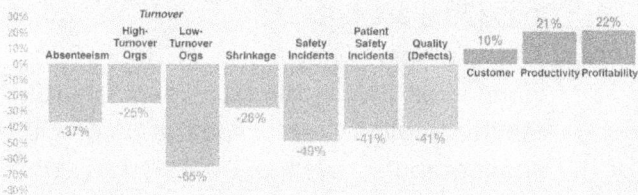

EMPLOYEE ENGAGEMENT AFFECTS KEY BUSINESS OUTCOMES

Work units in the top quartile in employee engagement outperform bottom-quartile units by 10% on customer ratings, 21% in productivity, and 22% in profitability. Work units in the top quartile also saw significantly lower absenteeism (37%), turnover (25% in high-turnover organizations, 65% in low-turnover organizations), and shrinkage (28%) and fewer safety incidents (48%), patient safety incidents (41%), and quality defects (41%).

A highly engaged workforce means the difference between a company that thrives, one that just gets by, and one that teeters on the brink of disaster.

A review of prominent research on employee engagement and business performance revealed:

- Engagement does, in fact, equate to dollars. According to Aon Hewitt's 2013 Trends in Global Employee Engagement report, for every 1% increase in employee engagement scores there is an equivalent rise of 0.6 % in sales. If this statistic were to be applied to a $5 billion company with a gross of 55% and a 15% operating margin, a 1% increase in engagement would be worth $20 million to the bottom line.
- Towers Watson demonstrated that an OC where communication and change management are highly effective are 2.5 times as likely to be high-performing than those that are not.
- The Temkin Group found that 75% of companies with strong financial results reported high or moderate employee engagement, versus 47% for under-performing companies. They also found that engaged employees work harder than disengaged employees with 96% of highly engaged employees reporting they try their best at work, compared with only 71 percent of those who are disengaged.

Still skeptical? Kevin Kruse has documented no less than 29 independent research studies that demonstrate a direct correlation between employee engagement and performance.

Lest you have concerns that these studies are merely a "flash in the pan," studies linking engagement and performance go back for more than ten years:

- Towers Perrin (2003 & 2005) – engagement levels linked to growth in revenue and operating margin
- Hewitt (2004) – same results as Towers Perrin, but added evidence of "causal link", not just correlation
- Numerous studies link higher engagement to increased salesperson and customer service performance
- Towers Perrin (2003) – engagement strongly linked to employee retention
- Sirota (2004) – engagement linked to increased share price

Towers-Watson took the research a step further in 2011 noting that in addition to engagement, organizations also need to enable and energize employees.

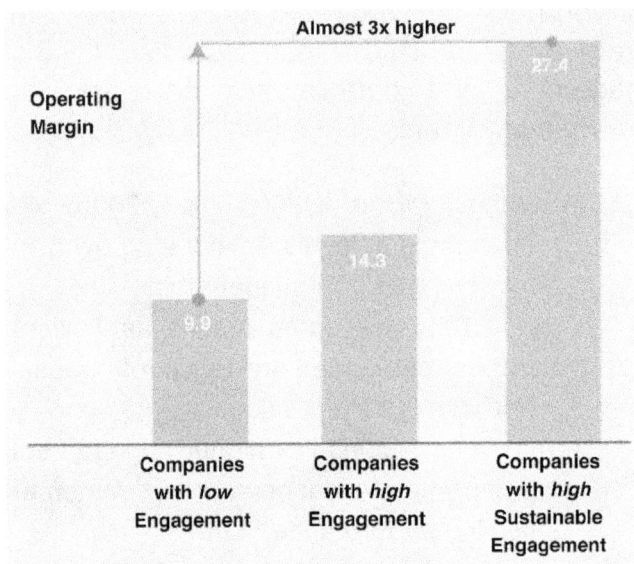

Enabling employees means the OC provides the support employees need to do their jobs effectively and efficiently. They also need to *energize* employees by creating a healthful work environment designed to support employees' physical, social, and emotional well-being. In other words, your organizational culture (OC) must focus on employee needs as well as organizational needs. When employees become frustrated because they do not have the necessary support to perform well, or the work environment doesn't fit their needs, they may be ineffective even though they are engaged. If this situation persists, it could lead to attrition or worse—disengagement.

A recent survey by Gallup (December 2016) shows that only 33% of employees are engaged and as many as 63% are not engaged. In real world terms, this means on average only one in eight employees is psychologically committed to their jobs and likely to be making positive contributions to their organizations. The 63% who are considered "not engaged" lack motivation and are less likely to invest discretionary effort in organizational goals and/or outcomes. Another 24% are "actively disengaged", meaning they are unhappy and unproductive at work and likely spend time disengaging their co-workers.

Dismal numbers such as these should have business leaders jumping on the engagement bandwagon. But the report revealed only 7% of respondent-companies rate themselves highly on measuring, driving, improving engagement and retention, and only 12% believe their organizations effectively drive a winning OC.

Further supporting the Deloitte findings is a 2013 Booz & Company study where 84% of the respondents indicated OC was critical to business success, but less than half believe their organizations have a winning strategy to do anything about it. While many organizations tout OC as important, only 47% of respondents indicated OC is a priority on a day-to-day basis and considered in leaders' actions. Only 45% of respondents believe OC is effectively managed and leveraged as a strategic advantage. A whopping 96% of respondents say some change in OC is needed and more than half (51%) believe their OC needs a major overhaul.

While these statistics are both compelling and encouraging, merely measuring engagement is not enough to improve results—no Hawthorn effect here! As a leader, you MUST take action to address issues highly correlated with engagement to turn engagement into results. But what actions do you take? The actions you decide on will be largely determined by your organization's values and philosophies which make up your OC.

Changing Workplace Dynamics

It's no surprise. The world is changing and to remain competitive we have to change with it including considering factors for success that were rarely considered before, such as OC. There are many driving factors for this change including:

- Employees, not employers, are in the driver's seat. In today's marketplace, employees have more information available than ever before—and they use it. Companies such as LinkedIn, Facebook, and Glassdoor now allow employees to share information about their organization in real time, including job openings, organizational culture, policies, procedures, corporate decisions, missteps etc. Using this information, current employees can quickly infect (positively or negatively) current and future employees.

- Technology is driving new ways to work. The world of work has become increasingly complex. Employees are working more hours each week, but many are working less in the office, connected in remote locations using technology.

- The need for rapid response, agility and flexibility, coupled with heightened technology is changing the way employees work together. The demand for employees to be flexible, continue to learn and develop, embrace empowerment and remain mobile is a driving factor pressuring every organization's OC.

- Employees are no longer motivated by traditional incentives. Today's employees are more focused than ever on making a difference and finding personal and professional purpose in their work. They are committed to finding and working in an environment that reinforces their passions rather than their career ambitions. This trend indicates the need for leaders to focus on the work environment and OC as a competitive advantage.

The majority of today's leaders are Baby Boomers trying to work with employees from four, soon to be five, generations all of whom are motivated by very different things. The one size fits all approach of yesteryear is no longer a viable option to attract and retain top talent.

Many leaders have never considered their OC, let alone how to leverage it as a competitive advantage. As a matter of fact, many leaders can't articulate their OC, let alone convey it in a meaningful way to others.

This is where the power of your OC really comes into play. The relationship between engagement, enablement, and energy is much like a three-legged stool where it takes all three "legs" working in harmony to provide the support necessary to be successful. What's included in those legs will depend greatly on your OC which then becomes the "seat" of the stool actually providing the platform needed for the stool to be useful.

What Business Leaders Want

As has always been the case in business, leaders are searching for anything that will give them a competitive advantage in the marketplace. Organizational Culture (OC) is embraced by leaders who recognize it as a sustainable competitive advantage because:

- Today's workforce is looking for more than a paycheck—they want a workplace committed to meeting their needs for belonging, growth, stability, challenge, contribution, and development.
- Following years of accounting scandals in some of the largest and most prestigious companies, such as Enron, WorldCom, and Tyco, organizations are looking to reassure themselves that similar unethical cultures aren't growing in their organizations and regain both employee and consumer trust in the business world.
- In today's competitive, global environment, innovation, and high performance are critical to success, but both depend on

employee engagement, risk taking, initiative and trust—all of which are reinforced either in a positive or negative way by the OC.

- Organizations need to stay a step ahead of their competition in a way that can't be copied. In Deloitte's recently released 2015 Global Human Capital Trends report, Culture and Engagement was rated by 3300 global business and HR leaders as the most important overall issue, edging out leadership, which was the leading issue noted in 2014. See the figure below. In addition to noting its importance, the respondents also noted their relative readiness, or lack thereof, to deal with engagement and culture as a strategic initiative.

Establishing the OC Needed to Enhance the Bottom Line

As a leader, your greatest contribution to your organization or team is to identify the elements needed for a strong OC and then create the conditions where it can thrive and live through employee actions. Your OC reflects the long term health and vitality of your organization. The actions of your employees and your leaders tell the true story of your OC. Whether it's good or bad, whether you nurture it or ignore it, your OC will impact your brand, your employees, your business strategies and your business results, which is why, if supported with intentional actions and leveraged as a business strategy, it can become your one true competitive advantage.

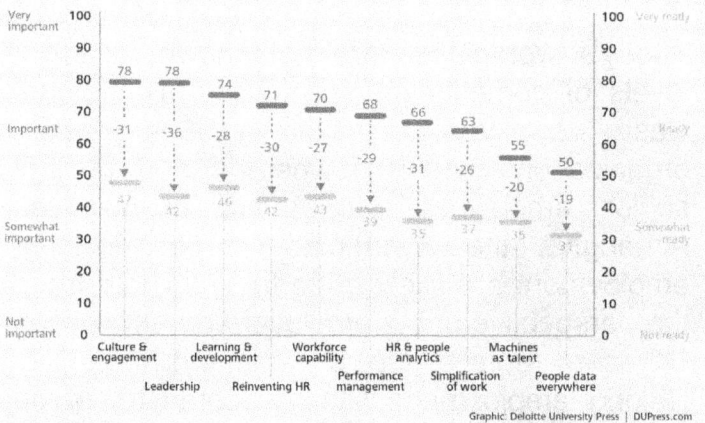

As previously discussed, your OC is simply how things get done in your organization. Behaviors, actions and practices, overt or subtle, which are routinely accepted and drive decision making and actions taken to achieve the business strategy. To be a sustainable, competitive advantage, your OC needs to be deliberately shaped around **The OC Equation**™ - Values + Philosophies x Actions = Organizational Culture (OC) and demonstrated through:

- A compelling purpose.
- A clear, concise, motivating mission and vision.
- Clearly defined and articulated values and philosophies.
- Supporting and reinforcing actions and behaviors that are celebrated, recognized, and rewarded.

Today's workplaces are not known for high levels of commitment and loyalty. That bond was destroyed in the 1980s when organizations began downsizing and cutting senior employees with years of service. Although the workplaces of lifelong employment are likely gone forever, both from the perspective of the employer and employee, OC can replace the commitment found in lifelong employment with the commitment of shared values, philosophies and actions.

Blessing White found through their research that organizations with a strong, well-articulated purpose and a long history of living their organizational values, experienced greater employee commitment than employees in organizations with emerging OCs. In addition, their research also demonstrated that more established OCs have less than half as many potentially disengaged or disgruntled employees.

In their ground breaking book, *Corporate Culture and Performance,* Kotter and Heskett revealed that, over a ten year period organizations that were intentional about living their values and philosophies and managing their OC outperformed their counterparts that did not.

- Job Growth increase 282% vs. 36%
- Revenue increased 682% vs. 166%
- Profit increased 756% vs. 1%
- Stock price increased 901% vs. 74%

In addition to these statistics, the Harvard Business Review noted research indicating that visionary organizations, those with timeless values and purpose, and agile business tactics, outperformed the general stock market and comparable companies in their respective industries. For example, an investment of $1 in 1926 in the New York stock market would have gained $415 by 1990. That same dollar invested in one of the comparison groups would have been worth $955 in 1990. But if that same $1 was invested in one of the visionary organizations with core values, philosophies, and a well-defined purpose using agility as a means to remain flexible in their tactical implementation of business processes it would be worth $6,356. While OC is critical to this type of success it is only one of many factors to be considered. Leveraged as a competitive advantage, OC can be the lynchpin for the other factors.

As previously noted, successful leaders make decisions based on facts and data. And in the case of OC, the data is clear—there is a business case to be made for establishing a supportive, positive OC. Strive to be an extraordinary leader by implementing the concepts and principles in this book and demonstrating that you not only understand the importance of a business strategy, but you also realize that what drives its success is your OC.

Getting Unstuck – Ten Things You Can Do NOW to Jump Start OC as a Competitive advantage

1. **Identify your organizational values and philosophies.**

   An organization's core values can be defined as those traits or qualities considered not just worthwhile, but that represent your organization's highest priorities, deeply held beliefs, and core, fundamental driving forces. They define what your organization believes and how you as a leader and an organization want to resonate with and appeal to both internal and external stakeholders.

Values are those fundamental, gut-level, non-negotiable beliefs and principles that predicate behavior (actions) and dictate how your organization does business forming the foundation for everything that happens in your workplace and how things get done. Core values set the tone for how decisions are made, what decisions are made, who makes them, how employees (yes, all employees) behave, how leaders act, how employees are treated. In short, an organization's core values dictate what actually gets someone hired, rewarded and even what actions get someone fired. Core values are literally the beginning, middle, and end of EVERYTHING your organization does and impacts every aspect of your organization.

It can be as simple as valuing productivity and creating an OC that leverages technology to create efficiency. In this organization, their primary mode of communication may be email instead of face-to-face meetings while another organization that values personal relationships and collaboration focuses more on face-to-face meetings rather than email or instant messaging to get things done. They want to create and reinforce teams who are deeply involved with one another. While this example may appear, on the surface, to be minor and inconsequential, many of the biggest blow-ups in an organization stem from small issues and challenges related to people interactions. For example, employees' expectations for using email or face-to-face interactions for communication that go unaddressed and continue to simmer until they explode onto the surface. As a matter of fact, I have seen high-level executives falter in new assignments simply because they didn't spend face-to-face time with individuals who were used to a culture of personal interaction, relationships, and collaboration.

Values often exist implicitly, under the radar of awareness, outside formal organizational processes, and create an unwavering and unchanging guide that quite literally dictates *how* things get done. Organizational values might be stated in single words, such as Trust, Empowerment, Innovation, Customer-service, Responsibility, Teamwork, Quality, etc. Or they may be value statements, such as "Recognize people as our greatest asset", "Deliver WOW Through Service", "Supporting team member excellence and happiness", "One Global Network," "Results, first - substance over flash", etc. Check out The OC Equation, Unleashing Your Employees' Passion, Potential and Performance through Organizational Culture for more information on evaluating your core values and how to get started. Regardless of how they're articulated, remember values mean little unless they are actually lived through actions.

Values are inevitably driven by people in power within an organization and that can be through either positional power or personal power. Values are most commonly established by the highest level leader in the organization such as the CEO, Owner, Founder, Executive Director, Pastor, or the most influential person reporting to that leader. Lower-level leaders who are respected by their peers can and often do establish and nurture their own values within a smaller segment of the organization such as a Department, Division, Office, Unit, Troop, or Pack establishing a sub-culture within the organization. These sub-cultures have the potential to take over the intended OC if the values of the sub-culture are reinforced and rewarded, making the original OC unrecognizable.

It's important that your employees' values align with your organization's values. When this happens, people understand one another, they understand what it means in your organization to "do the right thing" for the right reasons, and this common purpose and understanding helps people build great working relationships. Values alignment helps your organization achieve its core purpose and mission by ensuring employees are working together toward a common goal. When values are out of alignment, people make decisions based on their individual values which may mean they are working toward different goals and outcomes, have different intentions, and different priorities which can result in a culture "misfit". This can damage working relationships, productivity, job satisfaction, and even creative potential. Even if you can't see the misalignment, you most certainly can feel it.

2. **Define the organization's purpose, mission and vision.**

What's your mission, vision, and purpose? Are your leaders aligned with these? Do they inspire others to align with them? Review your values, purpose, mission, and vision regularly with all levels of your team and get them involved. Create an awareness campaign and offer opportunities for employees to engage in discussions about what they are and how the organization openly supports those things.

This is important because an organization that is clear, up and down the ranks, on who they are, what they believe, and how their actions reinforce those beliefs have a competitive advantage because:

- It allows them to attract and retain top talent that are committed to their organizations' strategic goals and objectives and are inspired by the OC to actually engage in the workplace— willing to go above and beyond to achieve results.
- It inspires employees to take responsibility for their actions and be willing to be accountable for decisions because they are supportive of the OC and actively demonstrate the organization's values and philosophies.

- It provides stability in the form of a fixed point of reference for decision making and actions.
- It creates a shared community where employees are connected and enjoy working together.
- It promotes a work environment where employee commitment, dedication and loyalty thrives by creating an emotional connection between employees and the organization.
- It aligns external stakeholders, such as customers and shareholders with the organization's purpose, values and philosophy so they can connect with and articulate what the organization stands for encouraging purchasing decisions based on their own values and philosophies.

3. **Create an environment where your leaders are your OC Warriors.**

We've all heard the phrase, "Walk the walk and talk the talk" but it's become such a buzz phrase, we seldom stop to consider how important its meaning really is. True leadership, leadership that inspires engagement and performance, is only achieved through respect and credibility. To gain either, a leader must walk the walk and talk the talk, so engage your leaders to be the protectors of your organization's OC. Here's some suggestions as to how:

    a. Hold regular HR-facilitated, leader-led meetings with employees at all levels of the organization.

    b. Share the outcomes and learnings from these events.

    c. Track feedback, answer questions and most importantly follow-up with actions. In other words, hold leaders accountable for how they are modeling the desired OC.

    d. Be market competitive with pay and benefits and take a BIG picture view of your total compensation program. Seek feedback from employees on the benefits that mean the most to them. Then customize your benefit offerings and other perks to suit a variety of needs and wants.

4. **Identify and focus on three programs designed to align your actions with your desired OC and engage employees.**

Be transparent and let your employees know these programs (actions) are specifically designed to reinforce who and what you are as an organization (values and philosophies). Don't be afraid to use recognition and rewards in creative ways to build loyalty and dedication.

5. **Provide employees with opportunities to gain the skills they need to succeed – today and well into the future.**

Consider what your top three training programs and recognition programs are and how your OC supports employees' career development opportunities. Do you encourage leadership development and mentoring as part of an overall talent strategy? Let employees know what their opportunities and limitations are.

Many studies indicate that millennial employees aren't specifically seeking leadership opportunities; they are content with just being an integral, valued part of the overall team. While this is noble, it may very well translate into a leadership shortage in the future.

6. **Make it easy for employees to do business with you.**

Review your organization's IT policy to ensure it provides safety and security for both employees and the overall organization, and then seek to fully understand how employees are using the technology or want to use the technology to be more effective and efficient. Where possible, move your HR and other processes online. Again, this is an excellent opportunity to engage employees in solutions that support the desired OC and promote higher levels of performance.

7. **Acknowledge the wealth of positivity that exists on your team, especially Millennials.**

Create opportunities for co-workers to engage and support one another and the organization. Provide a process so they can provide feedback and voice their point of view (POV) without fear of reprisal.

8. **But don't forget or de-value your Boomers and Gen Xers.**

Reenergize them with connection to the values, purpose, mission, and vision. Conduct open conversations and enlist their help and experience in discussions about institutional knowledge, valued organizational stories, definitions of values and philosophies, and the search for the illusive right "fit". Seek interaction and camaraderie between and across the generations and help them find mentors and counselors regardless of their age or seniority. Remember, it's no coincidence that Gallup's most highly correlated employee engagement questions is "I have a best friend at work".

9. **Share information often and early.**

Don't assume employees will automatically connect the dots between values, philosophies, and actions. Talk about and share the things your organization does and how they relate to values and philosophies that make up your OC. Create meaningful metrics and share the outcomes on a regular basis. Publicize your organization's achievements both internally and externally. People want to work for a winner and be proud of their partnership.

10. **Evaluate your OC quotient.**

Regularly review, promote and reinforce your values and philosophies and then "score" yourself on how well your action mirror what you say is important. Are your actions consistent? Do they promote achievement of the organization's purpose and mission and help both the company and the employees meet their needs?

OC and Engagement in Action - OC is More than a Touchy Feely Buzzword

At Royal Caribbean Cruise Lines, OC is no longer considered a "touchy-feely" buzzword, thanks to Tim Murphy, former CIO. When he took over the IT function, the IT team was considered a bureaucratic silo which did little else but put out IT-related fires. But in 2004 and 2005, through his visionary leadership and attention to OC, the IT department emerged as a strategic partner within RCCL and a key driver of their overall success, landing them on *Computerworld*'s list of Best Places to Work in IT.

IT and many other technical fields are not usually known for their touchy-feely side, but Tim's visionary leadership understood the importance of connecting with employees, all employees, and meeting not only their extrinsic needs, but their intrinsic needs as well. Connecting with employees through OC is critical to inspiring them to move beyond "just good enough" to extraordinary.

Leading companies have been using big data for a number of years now and measure innumerable factors related to performance. But for exceptional organizations, like 3M, they also realize that touchy-feely is what drives big data. At 3M, engagement is correlated with innovation, one of their key business drivers. 3M's own internal research found that business groups with more engaged employees were more innovative and produced more products than business groups with low engagement. Their findings also indicate that these increases in innovation resulted in high profitability and lower absenteeism within the business group.

Karen B. Paul, manager of 3M's HR Engagement and Measurement Center stated, "...when it comes to assessing the business outcomes of [employee] engagement initiatives, qualitative outcomes are just as important as quantitative outcomes. Success is when the hallways buzz with energy, when people come to work excited and when they are proud to be associated with your dynamic organization". As we noted before, engagement alone without the OC to support it for the long haul, isn't enough to create a sustainable competitive advantage.

What it Takes to Win

The evidence supporting engagement and OC as an undeniable competitive advantage and their impact on business results is undeniable. Yet many leaders have no idea what OC actually is or how to begin identifying, developing, and implementing a positive, winning OC. Their efforts often fail because they try to simply imitate what others are doing without regard to WHY they are doing it, and that won't work. Your OC is individual, personal, and derived from your values and philosophies. Don't be fooled into thinking you can simply identify your current OC and then pop a few perks in place such as free lunches, open offices (hotels), telecommuting, or flex-time to make people happy. This approach will end up costing you money and will have no lasting, appreciable effect on overall engagement or performance. As a matter of fact, your current OC may be hindering, not helping your competitiveness.

Effective leaders need two components to win in the marketplace: (1) A winning strategy, and (2) the OC to support it. Your untapped competitive advantage lies in identifying your current OC, articulating your personal and organizational values and philosophies, aligning actions (policies, processes, systems) and measuring results. You're on a journey and, like any business strategy, there is no quick fix and no final destination. Once you achieve one level of commitment and achievement, it's time to raise the bar.

Unstuck – The OC Equation™ in Action:

1. Visionary leaders inspire employees by connecting with them and addressing their needs.
2. OC is more than "touchy-feely", it's a strategy in its own right.
3. Leaders need both a winning strategy and the OC to support it to move from ordinary to extraordinary.
4. Evaluate your actions in terms of your stated values and philosophies and make adjustments as needed to live your desired OC.
5. Get on with it!

10

Infinite Ideas

Introduction

Is your brainstorming more like brain<u>drizzling</u>? When someone says "Let's brainstorm," do you just want to brainstorm ideas to end the meeting?

Too many times brainstorming sessions are just boring and unproductive. You're sitting in a meeting and the boss says, "We need some ideas. Start thinking about some ideas right now. Come on people, we need some ideas." Nobody comes up with any good ideas. The problem isn't that brainstorming in itself is a bad thing. The problem is that we don't do the things necessary to understand the true rules of brainstorming and to prepare for the sessions.

Let me give you an example – we are going to learn the two most important aspects of brainstorming with one directive.

Make up a story.

Hard isn't it? A story about what? You don't know where to start. What should you talk about?

Now, I'm going to give you another directive.

Make up a story about two kids walking through the woods who stumble upon an old abandoned house.

It's much easier isn't it? I gave you a starting point, a framework.

You've just learned the two most important rules about brainstorming and creativity. One, have a good challenge. Two, have some constraints. Just by applying those two rules, your brainstorming and creativity sessions would be a thousand times better than just the boss saying, "People we need some ideas."

If you've heard of brainstorming, you might have heard of Alex Osborne's rules of brainstorming. Alex Osborne, the inventor of the term brainstorming, is also the O in BBDO, the big advertising agency. He had these four rules. One of them is, strive for quantity. He figured that if you had a lot of ideas, you'd find a good idea. Don't criticize. Withhold criticism. Don't allow people to say negative things about ideas because what it's what we want to do. The third rule is, encourage crazy, wild ideas. Then, his fourth rule is to build upon the ideas. Try to combine ideas. If somebody says something, build on it. Make it a little bit stranger, a little bit wilder.

Research has proven that Alex Osborne's rules don't work well. You actually get more and better ideas from individual brainstorming than you do in group brainstorming. Why is this? If we look at Osborne's rules, we can see some inherent flaws.

First, Strive for Quantity - We instinctively know that a lot of ideas are just terrible ideas. What we want are some good ideas, even if fewer in number.

Second, Withhold Criticism – if a person is putting forth some really dumb ideas, or ideas that cannot be built upon, shouldn't they be constructively criticized? Offering helpful criticism can spark even better ideas.

Third, Encourage Wild and Crazy Ideas - some ideas are so wild and crazy we know they can't be implemented. Why should we waste precious time and energy trying to generate crazy, impractical ideas?

Fourth, Combine Ideas - This is the most useful of Osborne's rule - previous ideas can spark new ideas, but intentionally trying to build on previous ideas can add stress to the brainstorming session.

Alex Osborne's rules are good. They're better than nothing, but they're not as good as what could be. What he says isn't sufficient for having good brainstorming sessions. We've just learned about the challenge and the constraints. I believe there are six individual aspects, six sides to brainstorming, wherein if we address them all, we'll make our brainstorming sessions that much better.

We've all heard about thinking outside the box, but what is this box? This analogy came from that nine-dot challenge where the only way to solve it is to outside of the nine dots, or 'outside of the box.'

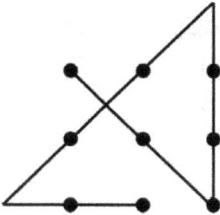

I've developed a box that contains the six most important aspects of brainstorming. I call it 'The Creativity Cube' and the six sides are the Challenge, Constraints, Criteria, Cultivation, Collaboration & Conflict and Creators.

Challenge

The Challenge sets the stage for all creativity activities. The Challenge can make or break the idea generation session. A good Challenge has three characteristics.

First, the Challenge must be legitimate--it must need to be solved. If a Challenge does not need to be solved, our motivation for generating ideas will not be there. How many times do you go into a meeting and someone says and get some good ideas, but you know that if you solve that, it doesn't matter, it doesn't mean anything? The Challenge must be legitimate.

Secondly, the Challenge must come from authority. If the group knows that any ideas generated need three levels of approval before they can be used, the team will not be motivated. If the junior intern says, "Hey we need to solve this problem," that doesn't carry the same weight as if the vice president says, "Hey we need to solve this problem." If you go into a brainstorming session with your manager, but you know that you then need to get approval from 3 other levels of people, and maybe what you come up with won't get implemented, and what you do probably won't work, you're not going to be as motivated.

Lastly, there must be a personal connection to the Challenge. If the team has a personal connection, they will be much more likely to generate good ideas. The third thing is it must be personal. There must be an emotional connection between you and the challenge, between you and the problem. This doesn't mean it must be your problem, but you must feel personal stake. For example, one of the groups that I'm involved in, we help the Nashville Diaper Exchange in their efforts to get diapers for low income kids. Now, I don't have any children. I certainly don't have a need for diapers, so this challenge for me isn't personal from that aspect, but I feel an emotional investment to the Nashville Diaper Connection because I've worked with this guy enough to see what his involvement is, to see his passion for his idea.

Once we have a good Challenge, we need to put it into a sentence, a statement that will inspire creativity. There are two aspects to a good Challenge statement:

One--Michael Michalko in his book '*Thinkertoys*' says to start every challenge with this: "In What Ways Might We..." This statement will help the team to think of multiple ideas. This phrasing invites multiple ideas 'Ways'. It exemplifies the personal nature of the challenge 'We'.

Two--there will be a level of specificity in the statement. Problems can be expressed more or less specifically--"In What Way Might We throw a party?" is more specific than "In What Ways Might We celebrate a birthday?" Choose a level of specificity that is no less specific than what you can implement. If you have authority in a department, don't make the challenge specific to the organization.

One caveat to your level of specificity - Don't go less specific than your authority. In other words, if you have authority for costs in one department, don't talk about, "How can we reduce cost for the entire company?" You don't have authority over that. Make sure your level of abstraction is no more general than where you have authority to implement. If you have authority to buy toner at a different place, you can say, "In what ways might we reduce toner cost?" If you have authority to change the amount of hours people work, or hire more people, "In what ways might we influence our labor costs?"

Constraints

Constraints are always present. No person or team has an unlimited amount of resources or time. Every problem has limits to what we can spend or how long we have to solve it. We call those limits 'Constraints'. Research has shown that the presence of constraints improves creativity--think about Apollo 13--"We need to fit these square air filters into these round air filter holes using nothing but the stuff on the spacecraft."

The Infinite Ideas process identifies Constraints for two reasons. One, we need to know when we choose or implement an idea that we have the resources to do it, and two, we will utilize the Constraints (I call it Constraint Busting), to help us generate more and better ideas.

There are three types of Constraints - Resource, Method and Time.

Resource constraints are things like money, people, knowledge and skills.

The second type of Constraint is method. Method is the manner in which things must be done. Some of that may be policy, or legal like HIPAA, Sarbanes-Oxley. There's a constraint of method, the manner in which we must do something.

The third type is time. There's a constraint of time, and that may be elapsed time, "We can only afford to do an hour's worth of stuff," or it may be a deadline, "This must be done by April 15th."

So how do we find our constraints? List the categories, Resource, Method and Time and think of the different constraints that are present. Now, we're almost brainstorming about the categories, but we ask direct questions. How much time do we have? Does this have to be done by a certain date? Do we have a limited amount of time? Do we only want to meet for one hour a week? How much money can we spend? Is there any kind of skill or knowledge that we lack? What is the skill and knowledge that we already have? List out what you know. You're not going to get it perfect. There are going to be constraints that you miss, and that's okay, but you're going to think of the major constraints present.

You're going to think of the major things: about resources, about money which is the big one, about time, about skill, about constraints with method. You're going to be able to know what those are, and if you list out 5, 6, 8 constraints, that's going to help us understand the bounds we have for the final solution. However, it's also going to give us those busters that we can then come back and use to create really good ideas.

Cultivation

What cultivation really means is preparing for the brainstorming session. There are two main tasks when preparing for a Brainstorming session: selecting the group and giving the group the Challenge, Constraints and relevant background information.

There are two types of groups: natural groups (such as direct reports or people with the same job) and selected groups (such as a cross-functional or multi-level team).

You may have a staff meeting every Monday morning as a natural group and you want to do brainstorming, so you've selected your group. The other kind is not natural or selected groups. That's groups that don't normally come together and we're getting them together just for this brainstorming or improvement session. Those groups can be chosen from maybe different levels in the organization, maybe different functions, different job tasks or job descriptions or different positions. They all may be in the same position but work on different shifts or report to different supervisors or are in different locations.

In one of my favorite projects, there were people from our customer base, my organization and vendors- all part of one group. We were all together brainstorming, doing improvements. No rule says people all must be part of your organization when you're selecting a group. We can select a variety of people, variety of different types, different positions, different organizations, whatever makes sense to give us a good diversity in our brainstorming.

It is important to give the group adequate time to prepare--to let their subconscious mind "cultivate" the Challenge, Constraints and background material. How many times do we come up with a good idea, hours or days after a meeting? Cultivating the mind will get those good ideas ready to spring forth in the session.

We want to give the group adequate time. We want to give them the challenge and constraints ahead of time. I hate going into a brainstorming meeting and nobody ever tells me why we're there, or they tell me why we're there at the beginning of the meeting and it takes me 20 minutes just to catch up, to try to understand what we're really talking about. We want to make sure that we provide the challenge and constraints in advance of the session maybe by a day or two or a weekend. The important thing is that we give enough time for the subconscious to work.

How many times have ever said "Ooh, that's a really good idea" while just taking a walk or in the shower, where your subconscious has been at work on it? The shower's always the famous place. We want to give people that opportunity for their subconscious to work before we get to the brainstorming session. I hate it when I have a good idea a day after the session is already over. It's too late then. I want to get it now.

When your subconscious understands what you're trying to do, even if you're not thinking about it deliberately, your subconscious is thinking about it and you're going to get great ideas just out of the middle of nowhere. If we can get everyone to have five or 10 ideas before they even get to the session, how much further along would we be? The other thing about cultivation is, in addition to the challenges and constraints, there's usually some kind of background information. Some data, some, "Why are we trying to solve this problem? Why are we trying to do this?"

We give people the challenge, the constraints and the background information prior to the brainstorming session; we're giving them all the information necessary to really have their subconscious work on really good ideas.

Creators

Creators are tools that help us with creative thinking. If you've ever been in a brainstorming meeting, even if somebody gives a good challenge and lists some constraints, your mind may then say, "Let's get some ideas" and your mind may come up with some, because you've phrased the challenge correctly. While you may come up with some ideas, you're not going to get great ideas just by thinking about the challenge. Creators are tools that help us with our creative thinking. They provide some kind of an input, a change of reference, something that helps us get different and new ideas.

There are many creative thinking or brainstorming tools. If you visit the bookstore, the library or the web, you will find dozens of these different tools. The idea is to apply them properly. I classify these tools into 3 different groups. One is challenge busters. With challenge busters, we're going to modify the challenge in a way to spark our creative thinking. The second group is Constraint Busters, where we look at the constraints that we listed out and modify those constraints to spark creative thinking. The third group is Generators - tools used in conjunction with the Busters to help us get ideas.

Creators are tools used to generate ideas. There are three types of Creators:

Generators-- help people pull ideas from their heads and capture them

Challenge Busters-- modify the Challenge Statement

Constraint Busters-- modify one or more Constraints

Generators

Many Generators exist for group brainstorming. The most popular example is classic verbal brainstorming, where participants speak ideas aloud and they are recorded on sticky notes or a white board. Classic verbal brainstorming, when coupled with a good Challenge, can generate multiple good ideas, but has some inherent flaws. Because the tool is verbal, quiet participants can be overwhelmed by louder more active voices and the highest-ranking participant can have too much influence.

In cases like that, a tool such as Brainwriting can help. There are many different versions of Brainwriting, but the general premise is that participants write their ideas on sticky notes, which are then gathered at the end of the session.

Since our idea generation session can't last forever, we need a way to determine when it should end. Two different methods can be used:

Generating for Time - in this method, a time period is established and ideas are generated for this specific time. Because the Infinite Ideas method has five separate idea generation steps, the time period should be short, not more than five minutes.

Generating for Quota - an alternative method is to establish a quota, either for the group or for individual participants. Quotas can range from 10 to 20 ideas. For the Infinite Ideas method, a quota of 10 ideas per each of the five generating steps will ensure at least 50 ideas.

Part 3 of this chapter will explain a seven-step process for generating more ideas using several specific Challenge and Constraint Busters. Either classic verbal brainstorming or Brainwriting can be used to generate and record ideas.

Criteria

How many times have you been in a brainstorming meeting and at the end of it an idea is chosen and you don't really know why? "Why did the boss pick Bob's idea and not mine? My idea was just as good as Bob's." The reason is that we haven't adequately defined the criteria by which we're going to choose the idea. We don't know why we're choosing one idea versus another. It's just some gut feeling that we may have or that everybody looks around the room and it becomes obvious that we came up with a list of crappy ideas to begin with, and so it doesn't really matter which one we choose.

It's important to determine these criteria before we start brainstorming. We don't want to just go to brainstorm and not have an idea of why we're choosing something for a couple different reasons. We want to use those criteria when we're brainstorming, but we also want to have the team understand what they're trying to accomplish, what they're trying to do. If I say, in my old example of make up a story, that one of the criteria is that it's the shortest story, well that's going to spark different ideas than if I say it's the longest story. Right? That may not be a constraint. I may not give you a constraint of 'must be less than two minutes' but I'm just giving you some criteria about why we're going to choose one story versus another.

Criteria will be present - we need to get those out in the open, to understand what they are and how they will be used.

Understanding the Criteria that will be used to select ideas is vital with every brainstorming session. Proper criteria help choose the best ideas and ensure that everyone in the session understands why certain ideas are chosen and some are not.

Each criterion must have the following characteristics:

- Specific--the criterion must be specific
- Relevant--the criteria must have something to do with choosing the right idea
- Testable--we must be able to evaluate ideas versus the criteria

Selecting Ideas and Using Criteria

The Infinite Ideas method uses a three-step process to select the best ideas:

1. Group similar ideas and name the groups
2. Evaluate the groups versus the constraints
3. Evaluate the groups versus the named criteria

The worksheet accompanying this chapter lists the criteria as:

- Solve Challenge - Does the idea solve the posed challenge?
- Meet Constraints - Does the idea meet the constraints imposed by the problem?
- Doable? Practical? - Can the idea be implemented?
- Cost - even if the idea meets a cost constraint, we may want to evaluate ideas versus one another based on cost
- Benefit - if there is a monetary benefit, we may want to evaluate ideas versus each other on the benefit
- Time - even if the idea meets a time constrain, getting it implemented quicker or by taking less time may be beneficial

- Passion - do we really like this idea? Ideas we really like get worked on and implemented better than ideas we hate
- Other - there may be other criteria we need to use to evaluate our ideas

Collaboration and Conflict

Alex Osborne only had one rule regarding group interaction - Withhold Criticism. We know that there is a lot more to group interaction that just 'don't criticize'. Groups need to learn to work together - to collaborate. They need a method to guide their thinking - to understand when criticism is necessary, when looking at negatives is necessary and when looking for positives is necessary. They also need rules to guide conflict resolution - when the group is having a conflict, how do they resolve that conflict?

The Creativity Cube leverages two methods for Collaboration and Conflict. The first is the Six Thinking Hats method developed by Edward de Bono and the second is a conflict management method based on the Thomas-Killman and Kraybill conflict resolution methods. Although a deep discussion of this side of the cube is out of scope for this chapter, no group creativity sessions will be productive without a way to manage collaboration and conflict.

The Worksheet

This worksheet will guide you through a seven-step process of identifying your Challenge and Constraints and using some Challenge and Constraint Busters to generate more ideas.

The seven steps are:

1. Identify the Challenge Statement and the Resource, Method and Time Constraints
2. Generate some ideas
3. Bust your Challenge by varying the Level of Specificity
4. Bust your Challenge using Morphological Analysis
5. Bust a Constraint by Maximizing or Minimizing it
6. Bust a Constraint by Reversing it
7. Choose the best ideas by grouping them and comparing them to your Constraints and Criteria.

Step 1 – Preparation

Preparation for the creativity session begins by taking the problem and determining its Constraints and creating a Challenge Statement.

An example of setting up a Challenge Statement and determining Constraints:

Problem - Bill's wife wants to do something for a milestone birthday on June 2. She has $100 to spend, can host no more than 20 people for 3 hours and Bill hates to be the center of attention.
Challenge Statement - In What Ways Might We... throw Bill a birthday party?

Constraints:

Resource	Method	Time
$100 budget 20 people	Bill hates to be the center of attention	June 2 3 hours

Infinite Ideas
using the Creativity Cube

Bill's wife wants to do something for a milestone birthday on June 2. She has $100 to spend, can host no more than 20 people for 3 hours and Bill hates to be the center of attention.

STEP 1: PREPARING FOR CREATIVITY

CHALLENGE

Based on your problem, create a Challenge Statement that is legitimate (must be solved), comes from authority and to which you have a personal connection. Choose a level of specificity that you are comfortable with and can control.

Example: In What Ways Might We... throw Bill a birthday party

LEGITIMATE	IN WHAT WAYS MIGHT WE... _____
AUTHORITATIVE	
PERSONAL	_____
ABSTRACT/SPECIFIC	_____

CONSTRAINTS

List the Constraints of Resource, Method and Time present for the problem.

	RESOURCE (MONEY, SKILL)	METHOD (POLICY, LAW)	TIME (DEADLINE, ELAPSED)
Ex:	$100 / 20 people	Bill not center of attention	Deadline: June 2 / Elapsed: 3 hours
1.			
2.			
3.			
4.			

Ideas.coach

Step 2 – Initial Idea Generation

The second step in the process is to generate some ideas based on the initial Constraints and Challenge Statement. Generate as many ideas as possible and note them in the boxes in Step 2.

When noting your ideas, give them just enough description that you can remember what the idea was about. When you are through generating ideas, number them to the left of the slash. We will use the idea numbers later in the process.

Infinite Ideas using the Creativity Cube

STEP 2: GENERATE! IDEAS

Based on your Challenge Statement, generate as many ideas you can. Record your ideas below. Number each idea, starting with 1 to the left of the slash.

1/	2/	3/
/	/	/
/	/	/
/	/	/
/	/	/
/	/	/

Step 3 - Challenge Buster - Level of Specificity

The third step in the Infinite Ideas method is to change the level of specificity of the Challenge Statement. Changing the level of specificity will spark new ideas.

How to use this Challenge Buster:

Create a new Busted Challenge by making the Challenge either more or less specific

Example Busted Challenge

Original Challenge - In What Ways Might We... throw Bill a birthday party?

Busted Challenge - In What Ways Might We... celebrate Bill's birthday?

Generate ideas based on the new Challenge and list them on the worksheet. Number each idea, starting from the previous idea number.

Infinite Ideas

using the Creativity Cube

STEP 3: CHALLENGE BUSTER – LEVEL OF SPECIFICITY

Modify your Challenge Statement to be slightly more or less specific. Write your new Challenge Statement below.

Example: IWWMW... Celebrate Bill's birthday

IWWMW...

GENERATE! IDEAS

Based on your busted Challenge Statement, generate more ideas and record them below. Number your ideas to the left of the slash starting with the number after the last idea on the previous page.

4/	5/	6/
/	/	/
/	/	/
/	/	/
/	/	/
/	/	/

ideas.coach

Step 4 - Challenge Buster - Morphological Analysis

The fourth step of the Infinite Ideas method is to use a tool called "Morphological Analysis." Morphological Analysis is a fancy term for breaking the Challenge into its constituent parts.

How to Use Morphological Analysis:

-Choose the original Challenge

-Break the Challenge into its constituent parts

-Brainstorm alternatives for each constituent part

-Combine the parts to springboard to even more ideas

Let me give you a simple example. In what ways might we go grocery shopping? Well, let's break that down; let's apply morphological analysis to grocery shopping. The different components of grocery shopping maybe transportation- how we're going to get to the grocery store and how we're going to get back. It may be carrying the groceries- how are we going to carry the groceries, how we're going to remember what to buy and how we're going to pay. We have 4 different portions of the challenge related to, in what ways might we grocery shop. Now, we can brainstorm; we can come up with ideas for each of those different aspects. Another example, we say, our transportation aspects of grocery shopping are: we could walk, we could take a car, take the bus or we could take a helicopter.

We've just come up with 4 or 5 different possibilities for the transportation portion. In what ways might our grocery shopping be related to carrying the groceries? Well, we could carry them in our arms or we could stuff them in our pockets, as well as we could borrow a shopping cart. There are all kinds of different ways. In what ways might we remember the list? We can write it on our hands, we could get a tattoo or we could use a smartphone app. We've just been able to brainstorm a bunch of different ideas about grocery shopping by breaking the challenge down into its constituent parts using morphological analysis.

Transportation	Carrying Groceries	Remember What to Buy	How to Pay
Walk Drive Helicopter	Shopping bags Pockets Steal a shopping cart	Smartphone app Paper list String on finger	Cash Coupons Don't pay at all

In a more realistic example, in what ways might we reduce costs? Let's break that down into different kinds of costs. Labor costs, supplies, communication, etc. and we can apply brainstorming to each of those constituent parts. Now, the cool thing about morphological analysis is once we've come up with, in this case grocery shopping, we had 4 different characteristics, we get 4 or 5 different ideas for each characteristic. If we get 5 ideas for each of the 4 characteristics, that totals 20 different ideas, just like that. We've come up with this whole list of ideas and different combinations and only brainstormed just a few ideas.

Applying Morphological Analysis to our birthday party problem, we may break the Challenge down into these parts:

Location	Food	Activities	Music
Home	Taco Bar	Karaoke	Classic Rock
Bowling Alley	Pizza		Classical

Generate ideas based on the new Challenge and list them on the worksheet. Number each idea, starting from the previous idea number.

Infinite Ideas

using the Creativity Cube

STEP 4: CHALLENGE BUSTER — MORPHOLOGICAL ANALYSIS

Break your Challenge Statement down into its constituent parts and record those below.

PARTS OF THE CHALLENGE

Ex: Location of Party	Ex: Food for Party	Ex: Activities	Ex: Music

ALTERNATIVES FOR EACH PART

Ex: House	Ex: Taco Bar	Ex: Karaoke	Ex: String Quartet

GENERATE! IDEAS

Based on your Morphological Analysis, generate more ideas and record them below. Number your ideas to the left of the slash, starting with the number after the last idea on the previous page.

7/	8/	9/
/	/	/
/	/	/
/	/	/
/	/	/
/	/	/

Step 5 - Constraint Buster - Minimize/Maximize

In Step 5 of the Infinite Ideas method, we will use a Constraint Buster of maximizing or minimizing a constraint.

How to Use this Constraint Buster:

Choose one Constraint and minimize or maximize it. For example, take a money constraint and maximize it to a huge amount or take a time constraint and minimize it to a shorter time.

Example:

Original Constraint	Minimized / Maximized Constraint
$100 budget No more than 2 hours	$10,000 budget No more than 2 minutes

Generate ideas based on the new busted Constraint and list them on the worksheet. Number each idea, starting from the previous idea number.

Infinite Ideas
using the Creativity Cube

STEP 5: CONSTRAINT BUSTER – MINIMIZE / MAXIMIZE

Choose one Constraint and minimize or maximize it. For example, take a money constraint and Maximize it to a huge number or a time constraint and minimize it.

ORIGINAL CONSTRAINT (RESOURCE, METHOD, TIME)	MINIMIZED / MAXIMIZED CONSTRAINT
Ex: $100 budget	$10,000 budget
Ex: No more than 2 hours	No more than 2 minutes

GENERATE! IDEAS

Based on your busted Constraint, generate more ideas and record them below. Number your ideas to the left of the slash, starting with the number after the last idea on the previous page.

10/	11/	12/
/	/	/
/	/	/
/	/	/
/	/	/
/	/	/

Ideas.comb →

Step 6 - Constraint Buster – Reverse

In step six of the Infinite Ideas method, we will use the Constraint Buster of reversing a Constraint.

How to Use this Constraint Buster:

Choose one Constraint and reverse it. For example, make a positive into a negative or reverse a "cannot" into a "must" method.

Original Constraint	Reversed Constraint
Spend no more than $100 Bill must not be the center of attention	Make $100 Bill is the center of attention

Generate ideas based on the new Challenge and list them on the worksheet. Number each idea, starting from the previous idea number.

Infinite Ideas

using the Creativity Cube

STEP 6: CONSTRAINT BUSTER – REVERSE

Choose one Constraint and reverse it. For example, make a positive a negative or reverse a "cannot" method to a "must" method.

ORIGINAL CONSTRAINT (RESOURCE, METHOD, TIME)	REVERSED CONSTRAINT
Ex: Spend $100	Make $100
Ex: Bill must not be center of attention	Bill is the center of attention

GENERATE! IDEAS

Based on your busted Challenge Statement, generate more ideas and record them below. Number your ideas to the left of the slash, starting with the number after the last idea on the previous page.

13/		14/		15/	
/		/		/	
/		/		/	
/		/		/	
/		/		/	
/		/		/	

ideas.coach →

Step 7 - Choosing Ideas

The final step in the Infinite Ideas method is to choose the best ideas.

Choosing ideas is a three-step process. First, we need to group similar ideas together;

second, evaluate the ideas versus our constraints and then evaluate the ideas versus some criteria to choose the best ones.

If we have had a successful session so far, we should have 50 or more ideas to choose from. Many of those ideas will be similar, even if they were found during different parts of the process. Grouping similar ideas will narrow down the number of ideas to evaluate.

Our constraints are constraints for a reason and so we must ensure that the ideas we choose meet those constraints.

Finally, we can take our ideas and evaluate them versus some criteria to choose the best ones. The criteria we will evaluate our ideas against are as follows:

Does the idea solve the Challenge?

Does the idea meet the Constraints?

Is the idea Doable or Practical?

How much does the idea cost?

What is the benefit of the idea?

How much Time will it take to implement?

How much passion or love do we have for the idea?

Are there any other criteria?

On the first page of Step 7, group your ideas. As you group the ideas, write the group number of each idea to the right of the slash. Name each group in a way that ensures you remember what the idea group is about.

Infinite Ideas

using the Creativity Cube

STEP 7: CHOOSING IDEAS

GROUPING IDEAS

Group the ideas you have generated into groups of similar ideas. Name the group and list the idea numbers in the space below. You can write the group number to the right of the slash for each idea you generated in the previous steps.

#	IDEA GROUP	IDEAS
1	PARTIES AT THE HOUSE	1, 5, 9, 13
1		
2		
3		
4		
5		
6		
7		
8		
9		
10		
11		
12		

Ideas.coach

Copyright Craig Paxson 2017

Finally, evaluate each idea group versus the criteria discussed earlier. Total the scores for each idea group and choose the winning idea groups for further exploration and implementation.

Infinite Ideas
using the Creativity Cube

EVALUATION VERSUS CRITERIA

Score each Idea Group versus the criteria below. Sum of the scores to determine winning Idea Groups.

Scoring: 0 = No, 1 = Low, 2 = Medium, 3 = High

Idea Group	Solve Challenge?	Meet Constraints?	Doable? Practical?	Cost	Benefit	Time	Passion	Other	Total
1									
2									
3									
4									
5									
6									
7									
8									
9									
10									
11									
12									

WINNING IDEA GROUPS

#	IDEA
I	
2	
3	
4	

Ideas.coach

Conclusion

If you take away one thing from this chapter, it should be this - set up a good Challenge and understand your Constraints. That alone will help you generate more and better ideas.

To download a copy of the worksheet, or if you would like more information about the Infinite Ideas method and the Creativity Cube, visit Ideas.coach.

Endnotes

Osborne, Alex (1942). How to "Think Up". New York, London: McGraw-Hill Book Co.

de Bono, Edward (1985). Six Thinking Hats: An Essential Approach to Business Management. Little, Brown, & Company.

Thomas, Kenneth W. (2002). *Introduction to Conflict Management*. CPP, Inc.

Gallo, Amy (2015). *Guide to Managing Conflict at Work*. Harvard Business School Publishing

Kraybill, Ron (2011). *Style Mattes: The Kraybill Conflict Style Inventory*. Riverhouse Press

---

Craig Paxson

Like you, process innovation expert Craig Paxson has seen numerous examples of ineffective and inefficient processes and process improvement efforts. Six Sigma? Lean? Kepner-Tregoe? Which methodology is best? Or is there a different, faster and easier way?

With over twenty years of process innovation experience, Craig brings a different viewpoint. As someone with Asperger's Syndrome, he has a unique way to view the world. He shares this unique viewpoint with his audience – showing them how viewing processes as a whole, and not as a collection of steps can lead to radical process improvement.

Craig helps process owners transform business processes into scalable, efficient, repeatable systems. He enjoys the challenge and process of innovation – using his proprietary "Process Innovation Canvas," and leveraging tools from Six Sigma, Lean, BPM and Creative Problem Solving. Craig has a unique ability to "see" business processes and translate that vision into actions to drive improvement.

Craig has developed the "Process Innovation Framework" — a unique tool used to map the entire business process, and generate innovative ideas for radical innovation. Combining thoughts from Lean, Six Sigma and Lateral Thinking, the framework prompts process owners to create breakthrough solutions in process innovation.

Craig's group creativity method — "Infinite Ideas" — is proven to help teams generate more effective ideas.

Craig has had success innovating key processes at companies such as IBM, Ingram Lightning Source, and Coventry Healthcare. He is currently a Process Innovation and Business Analysis Consultant at New Salem Consulting. He has a B.S. in Computer Science, and Master's degrees in both Business Administration and Quality Assurance.

Craig Paxson
New Salem Consulting
cpaxson@newsalemconsulting.com
615-722-7063

One Last Thing....

It's hard being the boss. Yes, the hours are long and the burdens are great. But mainly it's hard being the boss because you're the one who is always expected to have the answers. But who do you turn to for help?

Who do you ask when you don't have the answers?

One of the common themes from the 10 experts in UNSTUCK is strentgh in numbers. We don't have to have all the answers and it's ok to ask for help. Whether we're building up our referall network, connecting with our customer base, engaging our employees, or finding just the right person to help mentor us and guide our business. It's ok to ask for help.

With that in mind, we'd like to ask you for help.

Online reviews are the primary factor in determining which books get recommended and which books get read. We think the ideas in UNSTUCK are important and we want to get them into as many hands as possible. If just one idea from the book resonated with you, if just one suggestion helped you improve your business, if just one anecdote forced you to look at a problem in a new way, please take a moment out of your day to write an online review on Amazon.

It doesn't have to be a five paragraph book report, just a couple of sentences, 40-50 words, about how UNSTUCK helped you and how you think it can be helpful to others.

It will literally take just 5 minutes out of your day, but it will mean the world to us.

Thank you so much for reading and entertaining our ideas. We hope you've enjoyed, but that's not good enough. You have to put the ideas into action to make them worthwhile. Knowledge without action is just entertainment.

And it's ok to ask for help.

If there's anything we can do to help you implement the ideas, all of the authors are available for consulting and training, keynotes and workshops. Contact us at UnStuckBusinessAcademy.com and let us know how we may be of service.